TESTIMONIALS

The mental health and well-being of veterinarians has become a critically important issue in recent years as the profession continues to grapple with the challenge of rising suicide rates. **Dr. Kimberly Pope-Robinson bravely draws on her own experiences to help veterinarians— who may often struggle to articulate their feelings of shame and hopelessness—formulate a plan to achieve the "connected life."** Her ability to empathize with the reader provides a unique and powerful frame of reference, charting a courageous path toward balance and recovery.

—*J. Michael McFarland, DVM, DABVP*
Group Director Marketing, Zoetis

The Unspoken Life **offers solid, specific strategies for dealing with the unexpected events that come with living as a veterinary professional.** Dr. Pope-Robinson's stories are relatable, raw, and real. She reminds us that now, more than ever, we as ve   inary p f sionals are called to boldly and unapologetic   never know whose life you'll save simply by sharing. You might even be surprised to find that it's your own.

—Dr. Hilal Dogan,
Founder of the Veterinary Confessionals Project
www.veterinaryconfessionalsproject.com

"Connection comes when we recognize that we are each part of a larger whole." In *The Unspoken Life*, Dr. Pope-Robinson reminds us that we are not broken. Having been to a dark place during my veterinary journey, I can say that Dr. Pope-Robinson's message of hope resonates deeply, and **her seven principles of connection are a map to a sustainable career.** *The Unspoken Life* is a must-read for all veterinarians and professional caretakers.

—Jennifer Graham, DVM, DABVP, DACZM
Assistant Professor of Zoological Companion
Animal Medicine Cummings School of
Veterinary Medicine at Tufts University

As veterinarians and health-care professionals, we are driven to devote ourselves to the health and well-being of others. But inadvertently, we often neglect our own lives. *The Unspoken Life* will change how you react to the enormously damaging negative thoughts that diminish your spirit, cloud your reasoning, and drain your optimism. **Dr. Pope-Robinson's principles teach us how to embrace our challenges for what they are, recognize the enormously uplifting** connections we have in this world, and give voice to the value of our lives.

—Theresa Entriken, DVM
Medical Director, UBM Americas, Veterinary

The Unspoken Life is a powerful resource for veterinary professionals. **Dr. Pope-Robinson's principles help us to understand the choices and tools we have within ourselves and our worlds to balance the negative and positive influences around us.** If you are struggling with finding your "why" and need some self-care, guidance, and support, a reflective cruise through *The Unspoken Life* will reawaken the positive spirit and connections within and around you.

—Bob Murtaugh, DVM, MS, DACVIM,
DACVECC, FCCM
Chief Medical Officer, Pathway Partners

Dr. Pope-Robinson's raw and powerful stories take us on a journey that many in the veterinary profession can relate to, and **inspire us to rise high in life instead of sinking beyond reach**. *The Unspoken Life* will help you rise, too, no matter your challenges or moments of darkness, as we are all part of 1 Life Connected.

—Deborah A. Stone, MBA, PhD, CVPM
Founder of the Austin City Unlimited
Veterinary Management Symposium
www.ACUvet.org

The Unspoken Life is honest and inspiring. **Dr. Pope-Robinson brings to light the daily struggles we all relate to as veterinary professionals and builds a foundation for self-care**, transforming our reality from name-blame-judge to recognize-embrace-connect. A must-read for everyone.

—*Maggie Zink, DVM*
Halfmoon Valley Animal Hospital

People often choose to become veterinarians as children, when we are most connected to the animals around us. As we grow, life distances us from those connections—and for those of us who manage to get through veterinary school, despite the investments and sacrifices already made, we often feel even further away from the pets and animals we work so hard to help. *The Unspoken Life* **shares a familiar emotional journey and offers us a path to reconnect with the lives that bring us joy, and the passion that connects us all to one another.**

—*Ari Zabell, DVM, DABVP*
Sr. Director of Client Experience and Advocacy,
Banfield Pet Hospital

The veterinary profession has waited a long time for a book like *The Unspoken Life*! **With so many struggling to manage the emotional aspects of veterinary medicine, Dr. Pope-Robinson's book is a treasure filled with insight, wisdom, and heart.** Connection is key, not only within oneself but also as a way to recognize those around us, because we quickly find that we are not alone in how we feel. I recommend *The Unspoken Life* to every veterinarian I know!

—Julie Squires, Founder and CEO of Rekindle, LLC
Certified Compassion Fatigue Specialist
http://www.rekindlesolutions.com

Wellness matters. It matters for the personal well-being of practice leaders, veterinarians, and their supporting teams. It matters for practice culture and for delivering health care to patients and pet owners that is both empathetic and compassionate. If you are in the veterinary profession and are wondering if this book applies to you or your colleagues or team, yes, it does. **Dr. Pope-Robinson and *The Unspoken Life* have helped me step out of the cave of disconnection and into the light.** We must care for ourselves and each other if we expect to give the best to our patients, pet owners, and practices.

—*Dennis J. Chmiel Jr., DVM, MBA*

THE UNSPOKEN LIFE

Recognize Your Passion,
Embrace Imperfection, and
Stay Connected

KIMBERLY POPE-ROBINSON, DVM, CCFP

1 Life Connected

The Unspoken Life
Kimberly Pope-Robinson, DVM, CCFP
1 Life Connected Consulting

Published by 1 Life Connected Consulting
Copyright © 2017 by Kimberly Pope-Robinson, DVM, CCFP

All rights reserved.

1 Life Connected Consulting
304 Avenida Madrid, San Clemente, CA 92672
Email: k.pope-robinson@1lifecc.com

Limit of Liability/Disclaimer of Warranty:

Publishing and editorial team:
Author Bridge Media, www.AuthorBridgeMedia.com
Project Manager and Editorial Director: Helen Chang
Editor: Katherine MacKenett
Publishing Manager: Laurie Aranda
Publishing Assistant: Iris Sasing

Library of Congress Control Number: 2017902345
ISBN: 978-0-9986726-0-1 – softcover
978-0-9986726-1-8 - hardcover

Ordering Information:

Quantity sales. Special discounts are available on quantity purchases by corporations, associations, and others. For details, contact the publisher at the address above.

Printed in the United States of America

CONTENTS

DEDICATION

I dedicate this book to "Pirates Doubloon," aka Toby—my soul horse and the "balloon" who showed up at the most critical time, to save my life.

ACKNOWLEDGMENTS

There are so many people who have directly and indirectly influenced the 1 Life Connected message and movement. Although I can't capture everyone who has contributed along the way, please know that your support and value is present in this space, even if you do not see yourself noted below. The 1 Life Connected message exists for us all and is a representation of us all.

I'd like to thank my family for supplying support in so many ways as I started on this incredibly challenging journey—especially my husband, Jeff, who embraced walking into a world of financial insecurity and ambiguity solely to help others.

To Dennis C., thank you for providing me with the confidence to keep moving forward and for helping me look for creative ways to share this message and to make an impact on our profession. To Kristin J., you saw it all start at your parents' house on a lake and never questioned the value or reason for the path of 1 Life Connected, for which I am grateful. To Theresa E. and the CVC team, thank you for seeing value in this message from the start and helping to share it in so many ways early in its development.

To Jennifer G., I'm so glad we got to know each other, and I am grateful to you for being there for me along the way to provide me with the pick-me-ups I needed when the journey got hard. Jessica M., besides being the amazing running partner you are, you fill so many balloons and inspire me to keep this message moving forward.

To Robin P., Elicia J., Sarah G., Azi C., Jules C., and Lorraine R., thank you for recognizing the value of this message from the start and helping to get it out into the profession. To Anthea S., an amazing woman, thank you for providing me with the strength to push through difficult challenges and for motivating me to challenge the status quo.

To Alice V., without you I would never have made the leap to start the 1 Life Connected movement; thank you for believing in me and for being an amazing mentor. To Maggie Z., I don't know what I would do without you; I definitely would not know what "fall-off lighting" means, and I'd be lost on how to put those stupid lights together!

To Samantha L., your empathy for and connection to others is such a motivation for me to stay present and continually find ways to help others. You have given me so much through all our conversations, and I am grateful.

To Joyce L., who helped to open so many doors for the 1 Life Connected message to be shared throughout the profession, I can never express my gratitude enough. Thank you to the entire D4A team and leadership who work to live the message every day and who allow me to be a part of the team's journey along the way. To Robert T. and Kelly C., I seriously don't know where I would be technology-wise without you. Thank you both for saving my ass all the time.

To Matt S., I am grateful for the amazing creative brain you share with the world through your art, and how you never question my requests—only show up for them with your art in its full glory and beauty.

To Joann C., your undying support and love through everything—especially when Toby was lost—will always be remembered. You knew how to support me when a huge balloon popped with no warning.

To Michelle V., thank you for embracing the message wholeheartedly and for continuing to work to find ways to allow it to be shared with others. To Julie S. and Michael L., thank you for partnering with me and my crazy idea to provide a space for veterinarians to start moving forward in finding their unique paths to Recognize, Embrace, Connect. To Charlene W., I am grateful to you for believing in the message and helping to find ways to get it out there into the community.

To Steve K., you know I love you, and I am forever grateful for our friendship and all your support. To Lauren and Nate S., thank you for readily helping to share the message in such a creative and supportive way so that others can find their own path. To Heather L., I am grateful for your continued support and promotion of the 1 Life Connected message; you are helping to make a large impact on the profession.

To Michelle L., thank you for letting me crash with you during my early travel days, and then providing me such a great resource to share these ideas and thoughts with. To the entire VetPartners group, thank you for letting me be transparent and vulnerable, and for allowing me to take you on such an emotional journey while providing me with only acceptance and support.

And of course thank you to Katherine M., Jenny S., and the Author Bridge Media team, without whom this book never would have materialized. You made this process painless without ever driving the direction of the message, and you not only have helped me but also have enabled a message to be shared that will help many.

Finally, I would like to thank everyone in the 1 Life Connected community and all of those I share this message with. I value how you each show up in the message. You give me the power and conviction to keep doing what I do.

INTRODUCTION

The Dark Place

The day I almost ended my life started just like any other day.

The housecleaner had come the day before, so the house was freshly clean. It was springtime. The weather was warm. I can still remember the feel of the sun shining through the windows as I went through my usual daily routines: brushing my teeth, feeding the dogs, cleaning the litter boxes.

Then, all of a sudden, an overwhelming feeling came over me.

"Is this all your life is?" I thought. "Is this all you're going to do?"

I was in a fog. I couldn't see. I don't know what trigger put me in that place, but I knew something was wrong. I knew I had to reach out for help. I tried to call somebody, but she didn't answer. I set the phone down.

I had the utterly negative feeling of being completely alone, trapped, ashamed, and unworthy.

"You *are* alone," I told myself. "You don't know what you're doing. You don't even deserve to be here."

I looked around and thought of all my responsibilities. I wanted to leave my job, but I had put so much effort and time into it. So many people depended on me. I made good money for my family. But I hated hearing all the negative stories from the many veterinarians and teams I supported, day in and day out. My life felt as though it had been reduced to making money so I could pay for a house that was just more work to manage on my day off. I couldn't take it anymore. And at that moment, I thought, "I'm trapped. There's no way out."

I walked into my bathroom. I pulled some Vicodin, left over from a recent severe bout of shingles, out of the medicine cabinet. I sat down on the bench in my bedroom. I could feel the hard wood under me, warm from the sun. I felt the plastic cap of the bottle as it turned in my grip. I shook out a handful of pills. I didn't know how many I needed to take. Forty would probably do the trick. I poured more into my hand and counted them out, building up the "courage" to do this final act.

They say that if you just wait, the thought of taking your life will pass. That suicide is often a moment of intention.

"Do I do this? Do I take these pills and end my life? Or do I continue on into this abyss that is nothing like what I expected my life to be?"

A Life Unspoken

You may have visited this awful place, too.

Even for those who have never come this close to taking their lives, as veterinarians and caregivers, there are times when we get dark and lonely. We don't feel as if anybody can understand us. We feel trapped. There are all these obligations that have been pushed on us or that we have chosen, but that aren't, we now feel, what we wanted. We have made so many sacrifices so we could get where we are.

How can we not want to continue?

How can we not want to be veterinarians, when we have dedicated all these years and all this money to our careers? How can we not want to help animals anymore, when that's all we've thought about since we were four years old? We start to judge ourselves. We ask, "What's wrong with me? Why can't I feel happiness? There must be something I'm not doing, and that makes me bad. Why am I such a bad person?" At these moments, we can feel complete despair and disconnection from the world.

We care for so many lives. Yet our own lives can feel unspoken for.

So in some form, many of us have had the experience of sitting on the edge of that bench and looking for a way out. Around us, all we see is darkness and loneliness and a place we never thought we'd end up in—yet here we are. And the only way out we see is through drastic measures.

At the same time, we're aware of another part of us—the unspoken part—that doesn't want to take that path. We just don't know what other paths to take. We don't see any other answers available to us.

And we sit there in that lonely place, in that dark moment. Alone. Until the flash happens.

A Flash of Light

As we sit alone in the dark, a flash of thought passes through our minds.

That flash is of something we're connected to. It could be a family member, a child, an animal. For that moment, that connection becomes our whole vision. The negativity that was just in our thoughts can't possibly be our truth anymore, because we recognize that this being—this connection we have—is more important than the dark place. And suddenly, we can move from the dark into the light.

In this moment, we refocus on the positive, and we recognize that the negatives don't own us.

We look to that bond as a way to pull ourselves back out of the dark abyss. Which doesn't mean that in one moment—boom!—we're out, free and clear, never to return. But in that moment we connect to something, and hold onto it. Then another fleeting moment comes in. And then another, and another after that.

All of a sudden, these connections that we recognize bring us back.

We realize that we are all one life connected. And we are not alone.

The Choice

Many of us end up in that dark abyss because of our own choices.

But we don't have to judge ourselves for being in that place. We don't have to blame ourselves for it. Instead, we can simply recognize that the dark place is there. And instead of judging and blaming things on it, we can move toward embracing it, connecting with it, and—finally—coming out on the other side.

When we approach the dark like this, the direction we go from there becomes a conscious choice.

That doesn't mean it's easy. Choosing our path is an active process that becomes our willing responsibility for the rest of our lives. There will always be stress, expectations, and responsibilities, and our brains are hardwired to be negative. Most of us will have moments where the darkness tries to sneak back in.

The difference is that now we are able to recognize it and know that even though it's a part of us, it doesn't own us. Now, we have the power to choose to embrace other connections, to bring that positive part of things back into our lives.

We don't need to be fixed. We are normal people. We are in control, and we can move forward with our lives. It requires a conscious decision and effort to come out of that dark space. We have to open ourselves to the possibility that, even in darkness, the light really does exist.

And we have to give ourselves permission to take it.

Out of the Darkness

As I sat there in my bedroom, pills in hand, I was so ready to end it all.

Then, in that last moment, the image of my horse Toby flashed into my head. I had rescued him when no one else wanted him. Who was going to take care of him if I wasn't there? I thought about how much I loved him and he loved me. He didn't care about any of this other stuff. All he cared about was seeing me tomorrow.

And he wouldn't. He wouldn't ever see me again.

That bond was so strong it stopped me cold.

Then I thought about my husband finding me in the house. He had already left for work and wouldn't be home until later. Nobody would know to look for me. He would find me, and he would have to tell my parents what had happened.

My cat walked into the room right then. That was another unspoken connection that appeared when I needed it most. All of these connections brought me back for a second.

And that was enough.

I looked at the pills, and I said, "What am I doing?" I put them back in the bottle, closed it up, and put the bottle back in the cabinet. I was able to say, "Not today!" and know I was going to change this. I went to see my horse and spent time with him. And I was thankful I didn't kill myself that day.

I'm still thankful. I'm also thankful that I went to that place, because now I know how it feels to be in that moment of utter despair, to feel trapped, to feel as if there's no other answer. That dark space doesn't own me anymore, and it has even given me a gift: the gift to connect with other people who have been there, too.

My Path to Connection

I have been in the veterinary industry for more than twenty years. I speak on the well-being of our industry, and I started doing this because of all the interactions that I've had with veterinarians in a variety of different ways.

I've worked with veterinarians in both the small- and the large-animal sectors of the industry, in private and corporate practice, and in general practice, as well as in specialty and emergency settings. I've worked with individuals in academia, along with supporting the pharmaceutical world of vet med. I've been a top-producing doctor for a large corporate practice and a successful chief of staff, mentor, and coach. I worked in the industry as a medical director, at one point supporting as many as 120 other doctors in more than thirty locations with responsibility for a gross revenue stream of more than $50 million a year.

Basically, no matter where I go in the industry, I see the same things show up—a common list of emotions that come with the job. I've dealt with these struggles myself, both directly and indirectly. In my roles of supporting other doctors, I became good at helping and coaching people through the emotional challenges of being a veterinarian.

Before long, people started asking me to share my perspective.

"What do you need?" I'd ask when I worked with various hospitals.

"We need stuff on engagement," they told me. "Stuff on compassion fatigue. We need stuff on all the emotional crap that shows up with this profession. People are burning out. We lost an amazing doctor last year, last month, this week." Often, those losses were to that same dark place I saw that day on the wooden bench at the end of my bed.

So I started developing tools that supported people in that aspect of veterinary medicine. People in the industry started calling me "the emotions girl." Requests started coming in asking me to speak, first within the company related to the region I was working within at the time, then across the nation.

I recognized that there was a space for this. We were all

looking for a way to connect with each other about this stuff. This was the community so many people needed.

In October of 2015, I started 1 Life Connected. And our community has been building itself ever since.

You are a part of this connection, as well.

Your Own Bridge

This is not going to be a book full of hard facts, driven by data from scientists—all the typical stuff I used to be involved with myself, as a veterinarian with a science background. There's nothing wrong with facts and data. But most of the veterinarians and caretakers I talk to already know the facts. They spend a lot of time on the research.

The emotional side of our work is what gets neglected.

Some people might call it "touchy-feely," and maybe it is. But I've been given the ability to connect with emotions and verbalize them—to paint the picture that allows people to recognize how they're feeling. I've had a number of people tell me, "You make me feel normal. You put things into words that many of us can't vocalize."

That's why I wrote this book. To put into words the things that so many of us feel but can't vocalize. To remind us that we're normal. To help us build a bridge back to ourselves and each other—back to connection.

This book is not the answer to all of our struggles. This book is the starting place to help you find your own answers by connecting to stories—stories that you may recognize and live out every day.

We *can* step forward and take our freedom from the dark, without falling back into that hole.

So come in with an open mind, take notes in the margins, and pull out whatever resonates with you. In the end, recognize that this is just the beginning. Take the time to learn what you need to work on, for yourself. Find a place of balance between the negative and the positive.

Take the first step toward walking across your own bridge.

You Are Not Alone

There are times when we might find ourselves in a really dark place, alone and unspoken for. But when that happens, the first step back to connection is recognizing that we can get out again, that we have permission to embrace life instead of rejecting it.

The first step to pulling ourselves back is digging into the dark place to recognize where we are, so we can embrace that space and then begin moving toward connection again. Our paths take us in many directions, and if it requires counselors or pharmaceutical support, we will not judge that path. I have full faith that you can do it, as I did that day in my bedroom when I was first able to reconnect to something—anything.

I didn't find my message and take it out into the world as soon as I put the Vicodin back in the cupboard that day. I needed to work on myself first. I changed jobs. I moved and minimalized my life. I recognized the value of what living one life connected did for me. It took about five years after that dark moment, that unspeakable day, to decide that my life is not just about me—my life is about others. I choose to serve them and to help them find that connection again.

Today, I choose to speak that story, and share it with you.

I want you to know that you are normal. There is nothing wrong with you. You are needed, you are loved, and you are wanted.

You already have a lot of the tools you need to reconnect inside you. When you discover them, you will realize that you *are* spoken for. You are worthy. You are normal. You are not alone. You deserve to find that balance between positivity and negativity in your own way.

You are connected to this world. And you can cross that bridge back to connection. It all begins with just one step.

Chapter 1

The Bridge to Connection

Toby the Horse

As I shared with you earlier, the very first connection that started to pull me out of the dark place and into the light was the thought of my horse, Toby.

That bond grew from a place of depression. Around the time I met Toby, the complications from my form of Ehlers-Danlos syndrome (EDS-type 3) had started to develop—a clot in my leg, arches collapsing in my feet, my ankles starting to fall, loss of dexterity in my hands, and multiple joint dislocations leading to chronic pain throughout my body—and I had to go on disability and have surgery to correct the clot. I was never released from my physical limitations to go back to practice, and I became what I call situationally depressed.

Finally, I realized that I had stopped doing the things I loved.

So I set out to change that. One of the things that I knew I loved was horseback riding. I found a friend who was taking her daughter to a local stable and asked to come along for the day. As soon as I walked into the barn, the smell of horses and hay and even horse poop (I know, gross!) connected me mentally and emotionally to positive memories. I knew I needed to be around this more.

I asked Buddy, the stableman, if he had a horse I could ride. He gestured to two horses down the way. The first horse, Raven, was dead lame in the front leg. I knew I couldn't ride her. And then Toby stuck his head out.

There are moments where the unspoken connection between humans and animals is very strong. And at that moment, I knew Toby was my "soul" horse.

Toby was a thoroughbred off the track, very skinny and in need of some TLC at the time. But I rode him. He was the most perfect angel on that first ride. And we connected. Within a month, I told Buddy, "I want to buy him." He was not worth what I paid for him, but I didn't care. I wasn't "buying" a horse; I was ensuring that he always knew the love I had for him.

I needed that bond, but my connection to Toby went beyond that. I also needed the challenge.

I couldn't ignore Toby, because he relied on me. I was the only reason that he was able to go out—ever. If I didn't show up, then he sat in a ten-by-ten-foot stall, all alone. He forced me to show up, to be there. When I did, I felt better. Physically, I got energy and exercise. Emotionally, it brought me back to a place of peace. Spiritually, I connected with an animal. And mentally, I was a part of a whole community that was built around horses and the people who love them.

Without Toby, I wouldn't have had all of that. This is the power of connection.

What Is Connection?

I believe that we need connection for everything.

Everything has an energy, and every energy is connected. That energy is dispersed between each of us and brings us back to a whole.

Connection comes when we recognize that we are each part of that whole.

Without connection, each individual lives an unspoken life, alone and isolated, which truly is not how we were designed to be. When we choose to wall ourselves off, or become cynical or angry, or vilify everyone around us, that disconnect takes us to a dark, dank, scary place. There, we're unable to pull ourselves up out of despair, and we stop living.

So when we choose not to connect, we're no longer accessing any life force. And if we're not connected to any life force, how can we sustain ourselves? Connecting with the life forces that are all around us is what gives us the strength to breathe, eat, and live a fulfilling life.

When connection shows up, we recognize the totality of something bigger than just ourselves. We don't get sucked down into negative places of thinking that it's all about just our own being. We recognize that connecting with the whole energy of the world brings us to a place of peace.

We always have something else available to us other than just ourselves.

This chapter discusses building a bridge from name-blame-judge to recognize-embrace-connect, recognizing the sinkers and balloons of well-being, understanding negativity bias and neuroplasticity, and finding the path to a connected life.

Build a Bridge

All of us are looking for a way to build a bridge from the dark place to a brighter place of connection. That bridge really can be built. To build it, we have to move away from name-blame-judge and toward recognize-embrace-connect.

Name-Blame-Judge

Dr. Brené Brown, a vulnerability researcher, describes the concept of shame as "the intensely painful feeling or experience of believing we are flawed and therefore unworthy of acceptance and belonging."

This truly resonated within me, not only as a veterinarian, but as a human being. It's as though we are fighting every day to not drown in our own ocean of shame. Our fear of failure tugs us into that ocean. As we begin to sink, we can name the situation we are in. Then we sink further, and we want to blame or judge somebody. In order to explain the place we're in, we decide that, someone must have made a mistake. If we can just figure out who it is, we can release that negative feeling and it will go away.

For example, *name* is a way to say, "Those clients were jerks." Then *blame* would say, "They don't care about their dog, and they came in with no money." And *judge* would finish, "And I think they're horrible human beings. In fact, everyone is an asshole. I hate humanity!"

As we fall into the ocean of shame, imagine there's a serpent swimming with us, one who feeds off our cynical approach to a situation. I call this our "cynical serpent." We may feel the cynical approach is helping us to stay afloat, when in fact it is feeding the serpent, who then pulls us deeper into the ocean of shame and away from connection and life.

Those same thoughts can be turned inward, too. We don't want to live in this negative place, so we have to blame or judge *somebody*—even ourselves. Darkness pulls us back to name-blame-judge.

That's when we have to build a bridge across the ocean of shame.

Recognize-Embrace-Connect

The bridge is built with recognize-embrace-connect.

Recognize and *name* are very similar. You recognize that

you are in a bad situation. The difference is what you do with it from there. Instead of asking whose fault it is or looking for someone to blame, you move to *embrace*. The situation is just that: a situation. It is neither good nor bad. You feel what you feel. And your feelings are normal. You don't need to judge them; you just need to work through them. You embrace the place you are in.

After you embrace your situation, you can move to *connection*. You connect with yourself and the bigger world to move forward, to move past it. You might not be able to change the situation, and it might really suck. But you accept the emotions and mental state you are in. You check in with yourself to see what you need in this place, and you reconnect with the situation instead of turning away.

Name, blame, and *judge* are really easy. *Recognize, embrace,* and *connect* are harder. It's not easy to have an awareness of where we are and then choose to do something about it. But when we do, we take back control of our lives.

And once we have crossed that bridge, we do what we can to make sure we don't return to the negative place. That's where balloons and sinkers come in.

Balloons and Sinkers

To keep our balance on the bridge of connection, we have to understand the positive and negative forces around us. I call these forces *sinkers* and *balloons*. Sinkers are what drag you down into that dark ocean. Balloons are what you hold to keep yourself afloat above the ocean of shame.

Sinkers

Sinkers are the negative things that pull us down in our daily lives. As a veterinarian, you can be pulled into your ocean of shame because of a number of sinkers.

You have sinkers related to your clients and their pets. Sometimes there is no medical option to save a pet. Sometimes the owners have no money. You have the stress of not knowing how to do a new procedure that an animal needs.

Or you're scared to use a new medication because although it might help, you're unfamiliar with it.

Sometimes in this job, you have to use euthanasia as a form of treatment. You're not just killing animals; you're giving them the good death. But it can still be emotionally draining. Euthanasia is an incredibly complex sinker that could be a whole book in itself. You can follow the euthanasia discussion and find more information about managing it on my website at www.1lifecc.com.

You also have sinkers related to running a business, supporting your practice, or working at a hospital. You have the sinkers of work-related stress, as many jobs outside our industry have. You worry about not bringing in enough money, not being profitable, having to hire people, having to fire people, having to manage your brand and Yelp reviews. You may have hundreds of thousands of dollars in educational or ownership debt. And even though you went through eight or more years of college, people are Googling treatments and bringing them to you, expecting the answer they found online. And they may blame you and be angry when you can't give them what they want.

Then you have the sinkers of your own personality traits and your responsibilities as a human. Many veterinarians are introverts. If you are one of those individuals and you give out your "energies" all day long but don't do something to recover from that, you will be less resilient to the next sinker that comes along. Many of us are also perfectionists or described as high achievers. When we are not perfect in something—which happens every day—we feel sunk to the bottom of our ocean. There are other traits as well—being compassionate, analytical, or a workaholic; having a type A personality or being a people pleaser—all of which can threaten to sink us on a daily basis.

There is the sinker of judgment errors. You think you made the right decision with the limited information you had but later realize you did not, and your decision directly affected the outcome of that animal. We start this career with an idealistic vision of helping every animal we meet. Society even puts us, as caregivers, on a pedestal of selflessness. Then we realize that the reality is so far from what we expected. And the pressure of trying to maintain this unsustainable position can sink us even further.

It can get dark and depressing to think about all these sinkers, because they happen to all of us, every single day. The sinkers try to pull us under, deeper into our ocean of shame. And the only way to prevent that is to give ourselves permission to fill our balloons.

Balloons

Balloons are the opposite of sinkers. These are the things in life that keep us above the fear-of-failure line. They lift us up.

Each of our journeys is unique, and that means balloon filling is unique to each of us. There are four types of

well-being balloons—physical, mental, emotional, and spiritual—and you have to give yourself permission to fill each
of your balloons in your own way.

Physical connection. Physical connection is the actual
physiology of your body. This includes the need for
oxygen, food, and water, as well as the need to move
and be active.

Filling your physical balloon can be as simple as
asking yourself, "When did I last eat?" You may need
to go to the bathroom or put a jacket on if you're
cold. Maybe you need to rest more. Or you might
fill your physical balloon by going for a run, getting
your heart rate up, breathing harder, moving your
muscles, and getting your blood pumping. All of
these are examples of things that can fill your physical balloon.

Mental connection. Mental connection is the
exercising of your brain and mind. This allows you
to connect with the moment at hand and be mindful
of your current reality.

When I want to fill my mental balloon, I turn
off my phone and just listen to music. Music has
a great effect on a lot of people. It can calm you.
It can just put you in a different mental state than
where you were. I have my go-to Killers CD in my

car, which I play on drives when trying to manage a difficult sinker. Music can give you the mental drive to keep going. Of course, that is just one way to fill your mental balloon. Others can include meditation, working with a therapist, or prayer. You have to find what works best for you.

Emotional connection. Emotional connection is recognizing that you have feelings that can bring you both anxiety and joy. To balance on your bridge, you first have to acknowledge that the feelings exist and then move to understanding that they are not bad, so you can connect with them.

To fill your emotional balloon, look to memories and feelings that take you to an emotional place of being calm and happy. For me, that is being at the beach and around water. You can use your senses to evoke positive memories. A smell can trigger good feelings. Maybe a calming sight or sound helps you fill your emotional balloon.

Spiritual connection. Spiritual connection brings you to a place of wholeness. You recognize that you are a part of something bigger than yourself.

The spiritual balloon can be filled in so many different ways. It may be filled with a connection to God or religion, or through a connection with nature—anything that brings you to a place where you recognize that you are more than just yourself. You are part of a larger whole.

For me, being on the beach shows me that I am such a small speck in such a big thing called the universe. The waves wash in and out, and they never stop, no matter what is going on in my life. Fill your spiritual balloon with whatever gives you that sense of being whole.

Eaten by Dinosaurs

It's really important to actively engage with balloons, instead of just hoping that the sinkers and balloons will balance themselves out. This is because of something called the negativity bias.

The concept of the negativity bias is that our brains are designed to hold on to negative thoughts, feelings, social interactions, and traumatic events more than the positive things in our lives. In the psychology world, some people believe that this bias is genetic and dates back to when we were cavepeople, trying to work through the risks of what was going on in the world around us. The individuals who were able to focus on the negativity and see the risks very clearly were the ones who progressed and passed their genes on. The ones who didn't were eaten by dinosaurs (okay, humans didn't coexist with dinosaurs, but you know what

I mean), or they just died off because they didn't recognize danger.

When people say, "Well, all you need to do is just think positive thoughts," I think they're actually at a disadvantage, because they aren't recognizing the whole picture. Seeing the negative can be a good thing. We don't want to be that caveman who puts on a pair of rosy glasses, walks up to a cute dinosaur, and says, "I want to be your best friend!" That guy gets eaten.

We need to be able to recognize negativity. It's what we do with it when we see it that matters.

When we encounter negativity, do we hold on to it? Do we go straight to name-blame-judge and let it become our world, until it's the only thing that exists? Or do we choose to do something with it?

Recognize-embrace-connect says that we see the negative bias. We know it's there. We know there's nothing wrong with us for going there. And then we act. We embrace the negativity, allow it to be what it is, and then allow ourselves to spend some time in the positive. This moves us back into balance.

This reconnects us to ourselves and the world.

Fire Together, Wire Together

Because of the negativity bias, we actually need to teach our brains how to see the positive. This is where neuroplasticity comes in.

Neuroplasticity is the brain's ability to reorganize itself by forming new neural connections. As Canadian neuropsychologist Donald Hebb says, "Neurons that fire together, wire together." When you do or say something, certain neurons in your head fire all at the same time. The more often they do, the more natural that thought or action becomes.

For example, when you learn how to put a catheter in, at first your hands are shaking and you have no idea what to do with your fingers. But the more you practice, the more your neurons start firing together, and over time the muscle memory becomes unconscious: you can put one in while having a conversation at the same time.

The same thing happens with your thoughts.

Repetitive thinking causes your brain to get really good at thinking in a certain way. This is where the negativity bias comes in. If you think in that cynical, angry, negative space a lot, and you surround yourself with that type of environment, your brain gets better and better at thinking negatively. This is where we get stuck in name-blame-judge or, as I call it, feeding the cynical serpent.

The good news, though, is that neuroplasticity works both ways. Just as we've trained our brains to go to the negative (thanks to the negativity bias), we can actively train our thoughts to go down the other path, too—to recognize-embrace-connect.

I myself got really good at being cynical, and I still have to retrain my brain to recognize-embrace-connect through neuroplasticity. For example, I used to have really poor body-image issues. My whole life, I've had concerns about being fat and ugly. So when I used to see a beautiful woman with an athletic figure that I wished I had, I would try to find something negative to say about her to make myself feel better. "Oh, that skirt looks horrible with that shirt," I'd think. Or, "I can't believe she got her hair cut like that."

Then I discovered the concept of balloons, sinkers, and connection, and I knew I needed to change my thought process. So I started retraining my brain. Whenever I went to make a negative comment about someone, I'd stop. "No, you're not name-blame-judging," I'd tell myself. "Let's recognize what this really is and embrace it." And after a while, I not only stopped judging other people's bodies, but I actually got more comfortable with my own.

We can't just think positive thoughts to make the negative ones completely go away. We need to carry both, and because of the negativity bias, the negatives will always be there. When we retrain our brains to recognize-embrace-connect, it makes it a lot easier to stay balanced on the bridge of connection.

Across the Bridge

A lot of us think that we can stop the negative thoughts by not taking care of ourselves, by throwing everything into the sinkers to keep them from sinking us. We lose sight of the fact that the whole reason we don't sink is that we fill our balloons. Filling a balloon means "self-care," taking the time to fill all four balloons.

Just as neuroplasticity requires you to retrain your brain, self-care means changing your habits. In order to start self-care, give yourself permission to fill your balloons, and stay with it, you have to recognize and tap into certain principles inside yourself. Each of these principles puts you back in touch with your connections and helps you move across the bridge from name-blame-judge into recognize-embrace-connect.

I've found that there are seven principles that play a critical part in learning to live a connected life: self-worth, conviction, acceptance, courage, empathy, resilience, and vision.

Self-worth. Self-worth is important to becoming connected. You need to recognize that you are connected to a bigger universe, and your part is important to the universe. You deserve to be in that space.

Conviction. Conviction gives you the drive to keep growing, moving forward, and finding a way to stay connected. You may recognize that there is something more than you, but in order to stay connected to it, conviction has to be present.

Acceptance. Acceptance is important to connection because it allows you to embrace your situation. Only then can you move forward to connect.

Courage. Situations will come up that require you to take a path that is not easy. Courage is similar to conviction, but while conviction drives you to make the decision, courage allows you to actually follow through with action to reach that connection.

Empathy. Until you are empathetic with yourself, you can't be empathetic with others. When you have empathy in your connection with other people, you are able to live in their space for a time, and then move forward.

Resilience. Sinkers constantly come at you, so you need to be resilient. Finding a way to allow yourself that resilience will allow you to move forward to connection.

Vision. Vision is what you are, who you are, and why you are here. When you have the vision of knowing the deeper purpose within yourself, your path to connection is clear.

Each chapter in this book explores one of these principles—principles that you will recognize in yourself. You use each of them every day. When you recognize your core value—the "why" that drives you—you can use these qualities to find ways to surround yourself with balloons and speak your life's truth.

My "why" is defined by my recognition that I value life, and my mantra is "Life is beautiful." When I had to come to grips with my EDS—and the fact that I wouldn't be able to practice again—I stopped filling my balloons, and I was sinking.

And then I met Toby. I had the epiphany that there's more to me than what I do and how I make money. I forgave myself for not being everything to everybody. I realized that I deserve to take care of myself. And I reconnected with life.

You can reconnect with life, too. But how do you start?

If you don't know your "why," it can be difficult to pull yourself out of a negative place. In the next chapter, I'll show you why you are important as a part of a larger whole. Your self-worth connects you to everything.

Chapter 2

Connect to Your Self-Worth

Lost and Found

The first time I got my period was in seventh grade, at school, right in the middle of class.

I stood up to turn in a paper and noticed something on my chair. The kid next to me noticed, too, and suggested that I'd sat on chocolate, so I went with it. I quickly tied my sweatshirt around my waist and went to the bathroom. The shirt I had on underneath wasn't one that I felt comfortable in, so I went to the Lost and Found to look for something else to wear.

I was self-conscious, and I was vulnerable. It was such an embarrassing moment for a seventh grader.

Fortunately, I ran into some girls I knew. I was completely uncomfortable talking to an adult about this new development, so I reached out to them. We were all young and didn't know much about what was going on. But somebody gave me a pad. I found one of my old sweatshirts in the Lost and Found.

I finally started to feel comfortable again.

Then, just as I thought, "I'm going to get through this," the girls I had relied on suddenly turned and unloaded on me. They told me I was annoying. "No one wants to be your friend, Kim," they said. "Nobody likes you."

I ran home in tears. I told my mom that I didn't want to go back to school.

I didn't even think I wanted to live anymore.

What Is Self-Worth?

I don't know if I've always had self-worth. As a seventh grader, I clearly wasn't aware of it. But today, as an adult, I recognize that it's a value I need to have in order to stay connected.

We are not defined just by our superficial, material, or financial worth. There is more to us than that. Self-worth is the place of recognizing that our uniqueness is what connects us to the whole. Our value is an important factor as a part of the whole, universal unit. If we leave this piece of our unique identity unspoken, the whole unit doesn't exist as a larger entity.

Sometimes we get bogged down and lose sight of our self-worth. If that happens, if we don't believe we are worthy, then we disconnect from people. We start to think, "What's the point? It doesn't really matter if I don't show up."

But when you value your self-worth, you are able to stay

connected and not fall into a negative place. You know your self-worth is there, and that is where you find yourself.

Self-worth is a core value.

Instead of going to "name-blame-judge," I use self-worth to "recognize-embrace-connect" back with the world. If I recognize that my self-worth is not showing or is being challenged, I don't attack the person who put me in that challenge. Tearing down somebody else is not living for my self-worth. Instead, I embrace some of the core people who build my self-worth. Those people and that place of recognizing and embracing my own value give me connection.

To fully tap into our self-worth, we need to stand up for ourselves, take a stand against the status quo, set down the burden of society's expectations, and give to ourselves first.

Stand Up for Yourself

A key part of self-worth is standing up for yourself.

When I went back to school after that embarrassing incident in seventh grade, it wasn't easy. I had to power through. And there were other difficulties, too, like the group of boys who teased me when I walked home from school. My mom gave me a god-awful ugly haircut. And I had glasses, so the bullies called me "four eyes." They made mean comments and even threw pebbles at me.

Then one day, when we lined up for life science class, two boys stood on either side of me. They pushed themselves against me and called it a "body sandwich." They touched me, and I didn't want it. I didn't welcome that type of attention. Nobody around me stood up for me.

But that was my limit. I couldn't accept it.

I talked to a girl in my class who had always accepted me and told her about the situation. She took me to her mom, who was the dean of our school. Her mom said, "The way they're treating you is not your fault. It's not right." She gave me permission to stand up for myself.

She reminded me of my self-worth.

The dean told me that if anyone said anything to me, I should tell her. That made me feel safe because she saw me and believed in me and my worth, and she knew I could stand up for myself.

These boys would sometimes call my house and prank me with really nasty calls. The next time they did that, after my talk with the dean, I was ready. As soon as I heard the filthy things they started to say, I shot back with, "I think it's been made clear that you are not supposed to say that to me!"

They stopped in their tracks. They backed off. And they never said anything like that to me again.

So if you need it, I give you permission to stand up for yourself. I give you the "dean power." The situation that you are in is not your fault. You are worthy, and you have a right to speak up. No one else is going to stand up for your opinions, your thoughts, unless you do.

When I know that I need to stand up for my self-worth, I tap into the energy and support of the dean. I see her face and hear her words. That helps me believe in myself, because I believe what she told me. I believe that I deserve to be here and to be treated with respect.

You deserve that, too.

Saved by the Belt Loop

Sometimes self-worth means that you have to stand up against the norm, even if it's the way things have always been done. If you are not comfortable with something, you should not just stand aside.

When I was an intern, my responsibility was to do the anesthesia on all the horses that came through our clinic. The most dangerous times for horses when going under anesthesia are when you induce them and when you recover them. I often use the analogy of the most dangerous parts of flying a plane, which are takeoff and landing. Usually someone sits with the horse to hold it down, as best they can, while it goes through recovery. That way the horse can't pull itself forward and get up before it's ready, possibly breaking a leg in the process—something many of us in equine medicine have seen in our careers. I did this every day, two or three times a day, even late into the night.

One day, I turned away from the horse—and no one was there. I was left alone in the recovery stall with a

1,700-pound horse. If something had gone wrong, no one would have known. When I found the technician who had left, I told her that I didn't appreciate it. She said, "That's just how we do things."

I could have left it at that. But my self-worth told me, "You know, there's a risk here. And it's pretty high. Your life is worth more than that horse's life. I don't think this is something that you should allow to stand."

So I went to the owners of the practice and told them that we needed to change this process. I was scared, as an intern, about challenging the status quo, because that just isn't done. But I knew this was important, not just for me, but for everybody else down the road. It was for the greater good. And they saw the logic in my argument. Things started to change. I still had to speak up when someone would go to walk away from the recovery stall. By the end of my internship, though, it was standard protocol for a second person to remain.

A few months after we established this change, one of our externs was in charge of watching me while I recovered a horse. The mare tried to get up a couple of times, even though she was far from ready. I held her down, but she was able to lift and stumble, flinging me off her neck. The third time she did it, she threw me so hard and with such force that I smacked against the wall, my breath knocked out of me.

I knew I was in danger, but I couldn't move. It was as if

I could see everything happening around me in slow motion, and I just lay there sharing the space with an uncontrolled 1,700-pound animal.

Then I felt someone grab me by my belt loop and pull me out of the stall. Lying on the ground outside the stall, I could see the large, heavy door closing. Then there was a really loud crash. The horse struggled to get up. She was all over the place. The extern who had helped me said, "That horse landed right where you were. If I hadn't been here, you probably would have been killed."

If I hadn't felt that my life was of value, that I had a uniqueness that was worthy of being here, I might have let the protocol stand. But the value of my self-worth showed up in that situation. Let it show up for you, too.

As a side note for all those concerned for the horse, she did fine and made a full recovery. Fortunately, there were no broken limbs or skulls for her or any humans.

Set Down the Burden

One thing I've had to learn is that my worth is not defined by what people think of me.

In every situation, there are positive outcomes and there are negative outcomes. Negative outcomes happen all the time in veterinary medicine. For example, sometimes we can't give clients what they want because they don't have the money to pay for it. Then they want to name-blame-judge and get angry at us. They become an albatross that we have to carry, weighing us down with the societal vision of our profession. Society sees us as having an idealistic status, or it thinks that we're just in it for the money. It doesn't recognize that the business side of what we do needs to find balance with the caring side.

For example, imagine that you work at a grocery store as a checkout clerk. You're scanning groceries, checking someone out, and a woman walks up. She's disheveled, obviously homeless, and she doesn't have any money. She tells you that she has two children who are hungry, and she asks you to give her a loaf of bread from the shelf. If you just take the bread off the shelf, though, it's stealing. So you would have to pay for it yourself. What would you do?

You may or may not decide to give the woman the bread. But nobody in the store would judge you for choosing not to.

We, as veterinarians, don't get the same latitude. If people come in who can't afford treatment for their pets, and we don't do things for free, we are seen as uncompassionate. If we don't offer everything possible, even though we know we can't afford it ourselves without getting paid, we are told we're inhumane. And that is so far from the truth, because we know that it's killing us inside not to help that animal, often just as it hurts the owner. This is our beast to carry. I want to name-blame-judge the clients for putting me there, but what I also have to recognize is that unspoken connection that they have that is driving that response.

I myself have had to deal with this situation many times. People get angry with me when there is a negative outcome, because I can't fix it. But instead of getting angry back at them, I recognize that their anger doesn't necessarily have anything to do with me—they are just upset about the situation. I don't want to be insensitive to their plight, but I do need to recognize that it doesn't define who I am.

I remind myself, "I intrinsically define my worth based on what I do and how I do it." And because this one negative action by this person isn't able to sink my self-worth, I'm able to help the next one.

The path to sustainability in this profession is learning how to fling off that albatross of societal pressure. We have to get over letting society's vision of us define us, while also not name-blame-judging people, because that only drives us away from connection and deeper into the ocean of shame. When we find our own self-worth, we finally empower ourselves to set down the burden.

Serve Yourself, Serve Others

Without self-worth, we can't be there for other people. If we don't believe in ourselves as worthy, how can we show up for someone else? Giving yourself to others starts with believing that you need to give to yourself first.

When I first started 1 Life Connected, people told me that I wouldn't succeed. No one would care about my message. I wasn't unique enough. I wasn't individual enough.

Even someone within my inner circle whose opinion I value said to me, in an effort to understand my decision,

"You're going to be a consultant. What's unique about you that you can do that?"

I had to believe that I had value, even when some of the people around me shared their concerns. They were coming from a place of feeling protective of me as I made a major life change. Ultimately, I know they will always love and support me. But I also had to serve myself first by giving myself the gift of my own conviction in myself and what I was doing—by believing in my own self-worth.

And on the days when that was hard to do, I also gave to myself by connecting with people I'd worked with who believed in what I was sharing. They reminded me that I was making a difference, pushed me to get out there, and offered to help. You know who you are!

These things reminded me of my self-worth. I believed that I had a unique voice that deserved to be heard. I was worthy of sharing the 1 Life Connected message.

Because I learned to give to myself first, I was able to move forward. And 1 Life Connected has been showing many other people the value of their own worth ever since.

Recognize Your Value

When you look at the bridge to a connected life, you know that you have to fill your balloons to get yourself there. But you have to give yourself permission to fill your balloons, even when things stand in your way. Self-worth gives you that permission.

As a professional in the veterinary industry, you have to believe you have worth. You have to recognize your value so you can speak up for yourself. Say what you need to say in order to be here, to be present, and to be able to stay in this profession. Don't allow yourself to get beat up in that recovery stall. Don't let the things that other people say become your sinkers. Don't allow your life to continue unspoken for.

You are an individual who deserves to be present and who deserves to live.

Self-worth is the foundation of believing that we deserve to fill our balloons and live a connected life. But we still need other tools to continue building the bridge back to connection. After you recognize your worth, you need a reason to move forward. Conviction is the next step on the path to connection.

Chapter 3

Conviction in Connection

Where There's Smoke

In late 2006, I was chief of staff at a hospital for a corporate practice. One day, I was the only doctor in the hospital, and it was busy. I had four surgeries scheduled. Before going into surgery, I often went up front to check in and let the staff know I would be unavailable.

When I walked up front on this particular day, I smelled smoke. Something was on fire in our immediate proximity.

I told the receptionist, and she smelled it, too. It had an electrical smell to it, so we started pulling computers out of the workstations. I examined the lights in the ceiling for signs of an electrical fire. The hospital was in the back of a large-box pet supply store, and the reception area was out in the general store, so I looked over toward the pets for adoption and sale. Right in front of us was the bird exhibit area, with cages of hamsters and rats on either side. Cockatiels were flying around their cage frantically, so I looked up.

45

And on top of the aviary were red and orange flames, three feet high.

I immediately went into "save-the-animals" mode—probably a good indication of why I became a vet. "Evacuate the hospital!" I told the receptionist. "Get more people to help with the fire in the building. You!" I shouted at one of the pet store team members. "Get a fire extinguisher!" He didn't know where it was. I ran to the back to grab ours, but I couldn't reach the flames with it; the fire was on top of an aviary that was eight feet tall. I grabbed one of my technicians, Jackie. "Get a ladder and get the fire out on top of the aviary!" I told her. She never questioned my direction, just grabbed the fire extinguisher in one hand and the ladder under her arm and ran out of the treatment area, fully focused on her task at hand.

I ran back to the treatment area of the hospital, where my practice manager was preparing to start anesthesia for the surgery. I told her to execute the evacuation protocol and get all the animals out of the hospital. Then I took two other team members and told them that we had to evacuate the aviary right away.

The building was filling with smoke that burned our eyes and made us cough. We put on surgical masks to attempt to protect ourselves and went into the burning aviary, grabbing birds as they flew by and shoving them into any cage we could find. Then we went to save the rats, the hamsters, the reptiles, and the other animals attached to the aviary.

There were also rescue cats and rabbits up for adoption in the building, and they needed to be rescued as well. We knew that if we didn't get them out, these animals were potentially going to have severe respiratory distress or even die from the smoke.

We ran back and forth, from the building to the sidewalk outside. We ran up and down the ladder to put out the fire and remove the animals from the building. The fire crew arrived, and it was determined that one of my team members had to go to the hospital because of smoke inhalation. I felt something snap in my calf. But we all kept moving.

And we got all the people and all the animals out. No one died that day. We didn't even have any major complications. Or so I thought . . .

The Power of Conviction

What kept us moving through the smoke, flames, and injuries during that fire? It was the power of our conviction.

Conviction is the sense of something bigger than yourself. When that fire happened, we knew that if those animals died, we wouldn't be able to live with ourselves. We had a greater purpose. You have one, too.

Whatever your purpose is, it drives you to keep moving forward no matter what comes in your path. This conviction, this inner drive, is what keeps you in the present. It reminds you that you have an internal "why" to live up to that cannot go unspoken for. Even if something bad happens to you, you can tap into that purpose to keep you going.

Sinkers are going to try to pull us down. Conviction allows us to know that we can fill our balloons. Our conviction is one of the most powerful tools we have to keep ourselves balanced on the bridge between positive and negative. Even when things come at us that pull us a little more to one side, our conviction reminds us why we need to keep putting one foot in front of the other. Without conviction, when something pulls us slightly off balance, we're a lot more likely to jump into the ocean of shame and stop moving.

As I shared with you in chapter 1, my conviction—my "why"—is that "life is beautiful." I believe in living a beautiful life. Yes, there are always going to be difficult times, but there is beauty in everything. And there is more to life than just material things. The bigger picture is that beauty is in everything around us.

To own a strong sense of conviction, you need to find your own "why," stay true to your beliefs, and share your purpose with others.

What Speaks to You?

Once the smoke cleared from the fire in the pet store, I was left with bumps and bruises—and a golf-ball-sized lump on the back of my knee.

I figured I had pulled a muscle, but the pain didn't go

away. I went to the doctor, and he told me I had a thrombus, that I had thrown a clot in my leg. He referred me to a vascular surgeon, who recommended an urgent surgery. After the surgery, I had to go on medical leave and couldn't practice until my doctor released me back to work.

Then, as one medical concern after another materialized from my EDS, my doctor told me he would never sign off for me to go back to practice.

I had spent six figures and more than eight years of my life on education and training to be a veterinarian. When all my friends rushed sororities, went out to bachelorette parties, and threw bridal showers, I prepared for vet school, studying for this test or that exam. While those friends got married, had babies, and started families, I worked intense hours and committed myself to many sleepless nights of a different kind. I gave up my whole life for this calling. I sacrificed so much—only to be told that I would never be able to practice again.

And I had to come to grips with that.

I knew I wanted to be a veterinarian. I had just been running around, trying to save all those animals! But something in me remembered that what I really loved about it was bigger.

At that moment, I was forced to sit back and think, "What is it about being a veterinarian that speaks to me? What drove me to pursue that as my career?"

I love animals. I especially love them in their free

state—horses running free and dolphins swimming in the sea. I love seeing butterflies, birds, even spiders, where they're supposed to be in the world and in nature. I love water, and travel, and seeing the world. I love my family and friends and connecting with their lives. I like to run and be active.

At the end of the day, I believe in *life*.

I realized that even though I couldn't practice veterinary medicine anymore, I could still embody and embrace life. I support the human-animal bond and the concept of "zoo-eyia," the positive influence that animals have on humans. And I was still a veterinarian at heart. I recognized that the fact that I couldn't practice didn't take away the value of that connection.

So I moved into a leadership role within the profession, and eventually I started 1 Life Connected. That allowed me to show up and be present for other people, to help them find their path to connection.

Even though I don't work on animals the way I used to, I now help the people who help the animals. I get to promote the healthy lives of animals and people. I had all these negative things come up that tried to pressure me into giving up on this mission. But I moved slowly forward, away from name-blame-judge and toward recognize-embrace-connect. I realized that all the things that fill my balloons also feed my purpose. Because I knew my "why" and persevered, thousands of lives have changed for the better.

This is the true value of conviction.

One More Step

Conviction helps you keep going when you would otherwise give up.

When I first started as a medical director of a corporate practice, I was forced to recognize that my idealistic vision of what I'd be able to do in that position was far from the reality of the role. I thought I'd go in, inspire and motivate everybody, and help people reach the goals they'd always wanted to hit. Instead, my life was day after day of spreadsheets, numbers, and flash-report results of that hospital's daily interactions. It felt as though I was always going in to work to write people up, or fire them, or put them on a list to determine whether they deserved to stay with the company.

"Is this all I am to them?" I wondered. "I just push numbers. All they care about is how I'm going to force people to make more money?"

Then I went to a national leadership meeting and attended a lecture on moving forward through adversity. I went up to the speaker afterward, in tears, and asked him, "How? How do you move forward when what you believe in does not appear to be what everybody else believes in?"

He looked at me and said, "If you do what you believe is right, and it comes from your convictions, but the people you work for still don't agree with you and you get fired—is that a place you even want to be?"

That helped me recognize that my conviction is more important than the acts going on around me.

And I was able to change. The pressures didn't change or go away. I just saw them differently. Instead of looking at them as pressure to reach a number, I understood that if my actions inspired people, if they had an effect, that number would move.

When it came time to move the numbers for heart-worm-prevention medications, I made a new plan. I did something outside of what other people had done in the past. I came up with a creative idea on how to motivate change.

My leadership team and I collaborated to make a video to share with our market hospitals. I challenged one of my chiefs of staff to go outside her comfort zone and to develop and give talks in all our hospitals in the market related to heartworm disease.

And the numbers went through the roof.

I didn't just follow the path that everybody else followed. I came from the conviction of what I believed. And it worked in our favor, as well as in the favor of the lives of all the pets helped by the heartworm-prevention medication. But even if it hadn't, I would have been okay, because I had tried it my way, and I was true to myself. In the end, that's what keeps you moving forward, no matter what the outcome.

Bark for Your Heart

Conviction not only connects us to humanity, but to all living creatures in this world.

My conviction that "life is beautiful" is lived out when communities come together to support each other. One expression of this was a fun run that I helped organize called Bark for Your Heart, where people came together not only to promote health, but to honor the connections that animals bring to us. Bark for Your Heart was a five-kilometer fun run for people to do with their dogs. It raised money for a nonprofit that works to keep people and their pets together.

For example, if you were deployed by the military, you could lose your animal. Or if you went into hospice care, you would lose your pet. This group helped to keep people and pets in these kinds of situations together.

In the planning meeting for our first event, I said, "Hey, I believe in life. I believe in the connection between humans and animals. I believe in what we can do to help promote that positive influence of animals and people together. I want to go there. Who wants to go with me?"

And guess what? Everyone in that room wanted to go there.

Every single one of the forty people who showed up behind the scenes shared that conviction. They all volunteered; no one was paid to help. We had a marketing team, a team that made the course, a water team, one that designed the logo, another to deal with the website for sign-ups, a team to recruit people to run, and a team that brought in sponsors.

Our combined efforts brought close to 250 runners in all to the event—people who shared our conviction that the human-animal bond is important and worth fighting for. Conviction brought everybody together that day. We recognized that we were working toward something bigger than the individual. And the funds we raised were used to spread the power of connection into the larger world.

Live Your Conviction

Conviction exists even before you act on it, because it is an internal belief.

Even so, conviction lies at the heart of action—whether that's running through a fire to save as many animals as you can, finding a new way to move through an obstacle, or running five kilometers because you believe in something bigger than yourself. It's the fuel that keeps you going when the sinkers are trying their hardest to drag you back down into an unspoken-for life.

You've now taken another step across the bridge to a connected life. But how do you continue to move forward? By embracing your imperfections. Acceptance is the next principle and the next step forward.

Chapter 4

Accept Connection

A Cup of Acceptance

I happen to like Starbucks coffee. I also like the environment. As a child, I was always the one wanting to recycle. "Kim," my family would rant, "it's just *one freaking bottle*." And I would insist that, well, that was one fewer bottle in the garbage, landfill, or ocean.

What can I say? I'm the tree hugger of my family—and proud of it!

So when I grew up and started treating myself to Starbucks almost every day, I made a rule for myself: I'm allowed to get a daily Starbucks only if I use my own personal mug.

That way, I'm putting potentially 365 fewer cups into the garbage every year.

I stick to this rule pretty religiously. Whenever my husband goes out to get us coffee, he automatically asks me, "Where's your mug?" I even take my mug when I travel. The people behind me in line at the airport Starbucks tend to stare at me when I do that. They probably think I'm trying to get the ten-cent discount. (People, I'm paying four freaking bucks a day for coffee. You really think I care about ten cents?)

Then one day, my mug commitment put me between a rock and a hard place. I was traveling from California to Texas, and it had been rough. My plane had been late. I was jet-lagged and still tired the next day, but I had an event that started really early in the morning. Normally having that chai tea latte is just my daily habit, but that day, I seriously needed the caffeine. A colleague I didn't know well picked me up to take me to the event, and when I told him I needed some caffeine, he said, "Absolutely. I'll swing by the Starbucks."

Great, I thought. And then, before I realized where he was going, he was headed to a drive-thru.

At that point, I had a choice. I could cause a scene, dig around for my mug, and make this new acquaintance haggle with the drive-thru window for me while we held up the line. Or I could accept the unusual situation just this once and take the paper cup.

"Kim, it's okay," I told myself. "Just take the cup this time, and next time you'll get back on track."

I took the paper cup. The world didn't end. Later, after I got to know my colleague better, I told him this story, and now we joke about it. That day, my acceptance of an uncomfortable situation became the beginning of a strong working relationship.

Acceptance in Action

Acceptance is a big part of working as a veterinarian. When we recognize that there's a sinker in our orbit making us feel powerless and unspoken for, acceptance is what we use to embrace it and move forward.

If we don't practice acceptance, we can easily jump to a place of name-blame-judge, which leaves us hanging on to the negative. Acceptance allows us to grab ahold of the light on the positive side of things so that we maintain a balance.

I truly believe that self-forgiveness—a main part of acceptance—is the foundation of why I was able to have a sustainable career in veterinary medicine. Self-forgiveness, accepting our imperfections, and accepting every part of our jobs as veterinarians are the three things we need in this industry for total acceptance.

In this chapter, I'll explain each of these parts of acceptance and share how I've practiced them in my career.

The End of the Line

Learning to forgive ourselves for our mistakes is an important part of being a veterinarian. Sometimes, people will ask more of us than we can physically or mentally give. Sometimes, we're going to do things we don't mean to do. But that doesn't define who we are.

I once worked with a client whom we'll call Teresa. Teresa had a cat and a dog she brought to me for veterinary care, and I discovered, while building that relationship with her, that we liked to do a lot of the same things. She and her black Labrador, we'll call him Stanley, would hike, go to the lake, and do other things to stay active and be out in nature. She got out there, saw the world, and lived her beliefs. We had those things in common, and eventually we built a friendship on them.

I was there for Teresa as her dog got older and began needing therapies related to aging. When I moved to a new hospital, Teresa followed me and soon after started her own spa business in the same neighborhood.

I continued to help her out with Stanley, but eventually life took its toll, and Teresa had to say her goodbyes to him. It was hard for us both, but we worked through it together. We bonded even more, and although we never interacted outside the hospital setting, our relationship became more personal than just a basic client and doctor relationship.

After her dog passed, I saw Teresa a little less because she didn't need to bring her cat in as regularly as she had Stanley. But one day, she frantically called the office. "Please," she told my receptionist, "my cat has been hit by a car. His leg is broken. I need to bring him in to see Dr. Pope right away."

Now on this particular day, I needed to leave early for a personal obligation. It was my husband's birthday party, and I knew that if I was late another time to this kind of thing, my family and friends would disown me. I had missed many social events throughout my training and early years of practice. There was a lot of pressure to get out on time and be there.

But Teresa insisted on seeing me, and my receptionist didn't know about my obligation, so she told her to come right down. I had my purse on my arm and keys in hand, as I was already supposed to be on my way home. The shame of failing my husband once again started to creep in. Still, I didn't feel I could leave.

By the time Teresa arrived with her cat, I was in a really negative place.

I couldn't believe I was missing another family event. During the appointment, I wasn't as careful, empathetic, or present as I normally would be. Once, I went to move the cat and he screamed out in pain. My heart, hearing his painful cry, dropped.

I could see the concern and disappointment on Teresa's face.

Right then, I forgot everything going on at home, and the situation in front of me became my number one priority. I carefully stabilized the leg, prescribed pain medication, and referred Teresa and her cat to the emergency clinic for surgical correction.

But it was too late. I was sure that my six years of friendship with Teresa were lost in those few seconds of carelessness and loss of focus. I didn't hear from her for a while afterward, and that seemed to be the proof.

Then, right around the time the cat should have come back in for a checkup, I got a call from Teresa's fiancé.

I was sure she was having him call to let me know that she wouldn't be working with our office anymore. Instead, he told me that Teresa had recently been killed in a bicycle accident. I was stunned. She had been totally full of life, and I saw myself in her. I could not believe I was never going to see her again!

In that moment, I also realized I was never going to get to say "I'm sorry" to her for how I had handled that one appointment. Our last interaction would always be one of disappointment. Of disconnect.

But her fiancé wasn't finished. "Kim," he said, "I'm calling because I want you to know that Teresa thought the world of you." I closed my eyes, and the tears just began to flow. I barely was able to express my condolences. I still cry when I think about Teresa.

It was hard to accept her death. But those words ultimately

helped me understand that one appointment with her didn't define me. That wasn't who I was to her in the end.

I had to come to grips with the fact that my actions that day did not define my compassion, or my connection with veterinary medicine, or my love for animals or Teresa. She still saw the value in me as a doctor and friend, and I had to forgive myself. Acceptance allowed me to move forward so that I could keep helping many other people and their pets. I will forever hold Teresa in my heart.

Soap Cookies

To have true acceptance, you have to embrace your imperfections.

One holiday season, I wanted to recognize my staff's hard work by baking them cookies. I decided to do the same thing for the senior veterinary students at the local vet college, my alma mater. Pets don't know not to get sick around Thanksgiving and Christmas, so these students were working through the holidays to support our clients. I wanted to share my appreciation of that.

I spent three full days preparing and baking treats. We're talking multiple batches of banana bread, zucchini bread, chocolate chip cookies, peanut butter cookies, frosted sugar cookies, brownies, Rice Krispies treats—I mean *everything*.

Not only did I bake them, but I also individually wrapped each dessert. I didn't want anyone with a particular allergy to eat anything he or she didn't mean to eat. Then I made little labels for each treat, so everyone knew what they were getting.

The student representatives for the school, Jovi and Rachel, assisted me with delivering these wonderful baked goodies that had taken three entire days to create. My leadership team and I took time to plan our entire approach for spreading the cheer to everyone within our market hospitals. Keep in mind that I was a medical director and, at the time, supported seventeen hospitals, sixty doctors, and hundreds of other staff members. We had a lot of ground to cover.

When we were finally all set, I dressed my dog up like a reindeer, packed my bag with the goodies, and made my way out on the delivery route.

Partway through the day of the Reindeer Run (as we called it), I got a call from Jovi at the local college. She had delivered the treats to the senior students and faculty at the vet school. "Dr. Pope, I'm getting some complaints from the students," she told me. "The cookies, well . . . they taste like soap."

I thought Jovi was crazy.

I went straight into name-blame-judge mode and assumed Jovi or Rachel must have accidentally contaminated the treats when they helped set them up. After all, I'd met up with Rachel earlier in the day and transferred the school's delivery to her car, so that she could take them with her to school. She or Jovi must have had something soapy in their car, right?

When I got to the next hospital for delivery, I vented to the staff. "The vet students think we are trying to poison them with soapy treats," I ranted. "I have to try the cookies for myself." I unwrapped one and took a bite.

Sure enough, it tasted like soap.

"Oh no," I thought. I warned the other hospitals I'd been to and called Jovi back and told her to trash all the cookies.

All my excitement about the Reindeer Run was lost. I still couldn't believe it. What had happened? I went straight home to figure out where I'd made a mistake.

Once I got there, my husband noticed that the Saran Wrap that was still sitting on the kitchen counter, which I had used to package the treats, smelled like laundry detergent. Instead of the kitchen wrap, I'd used the wrap we stored in the laundry room near the fabric softener sheets.

Wow. Three backbreaking days of baking . . . for soap cookies.

"I'm a horrible person," I thought as the downward spiral of this sinker kicked in. "Corporate practices already have a bad reputation, and here I am, promoting that theory. It probably looks like I was totally trying to kill these people."

But I had to learn to accept this imperfection. I did it by recognizing that my mistake didn't come from a place of negativity. It wasn't as if I had made the cookies and then said, "I want to screw with everybody. I'll put soap in them." It just happened, unintentionally. I had to accept the fact that it was just a mistake. By doing that, I was able to learn from it.

I still bake treats for people. Now, I just wrap them in something other than (easily contaminated) Saran Wrap. And I keep that "something" out of the laundry room.

The Freedom of Acceptance

A vet's job isn't an easy one. Sometimes we make mistakes, and sometimes we have to deal with difficult scenarios. When people ask me what it's like to be a veterinarian and why it's so hard, these are the things I reference. Not many jobs require the same kind of connected relationships with animals and people. Pets and their owners trust in us. With that comes a lot of responsibility and pressure.

We have less of a job and more of a lifestyle, as honoring the human-animal bond is not just something we leave at the door when we hang up our lab coats.

But if you can learn to forgive yourself for your mistakes, accept your imperfections, and embrace all aspects of the job, you'll find yourself much less overwhelmed by everything that goes into it. You'll recognize that your own life is as valuable as the ones that you are helping.

You'll be able to keep building your bridge of connection, one plank and one day at a time.

Once you accept things for what they are, you can use your clear perception to grow and focus on what's important. In the next chapter, we'll look at courage—the force you need to stand behind your convictions and move forward in your career the way you choose to.

Chapter 5

The Courage to Connect

Tough Mudders

I run Tough Mudders.

Tough Mudders are eight- to ten-mile, military-style obstacle courses. I run them because they restore my faith in humanity, and also because they restore my faith in myself. They are just as much mental as they are physical. One of the obstacles in a Tough Mudder course is the Arctic Enema, where you have to jump into a giant dumpster of ice water. Another obstacle is called the Birth Canal, which is a tunnel with water sitting on a tarp on top of you.

It would be an understatement to say that it takes a little courage to do some of these obstacles.

Tough Mudders are not timed, and no one is forced to do any of the obstacles. With my chronic connective-tissue disorder, I dislocate and subluxate my joints really easily, so there are many obstacles I just physically cannot do. I have to recognize my limitations, even when it makes me angry.

There was one obstacle, though, that I really, really wanted to do, no matter what. I wanted to beat the King of the Swingers.

For King of the Swingers, you start on a plank two stories up. Then you run and jump to grab a trapeze, swing out, let go of the bar and reach to ring a bell, and then dead fall into deep, cold, muddy water.

Because of my EDS, it took active courage for me to take this obstacle on and say, "What do I need in order to be able to do this?" My right shoulder joint was so unstable that it could have dislocated while I slept, so I had to be very strategic in my approach. First, I had to work really hard to build up my strength. Then, I asked a friend to go through the obstacle once for me. Afterward, she was able to tell me how it works, how she did it, and exactly what to do to protect my shoulder.

I knew I had to try. But I also knew that if I didn't do it perfectly, I would hurt my shoulder, and I would fail with drastic consequences. I wasn't scared of the height. I wasn't scared of jumping off and grabbing the trapeze. I was scared of hurting myself; the pain from doing so in the past is forever engraved on my brain.

I went through with it anyway.

I put all of my focus on the act of what I was doing. I had 100 percent of my concentration on my muscles, focused only on protecting my right shoulder. I recognized the risk I was about to take, but I also knew what I needed to do to manage that risk. And I had the courage to take action.

So I jumped. I grabbed the bar, swung out, let go, and fell in the water. I didn't come close to ringing the bell, but I was ecstatic because I didn't hurt my shoulder.

At that moment, I proved to myself that I could do it. And because I was able to do it, I proved that EDS does not own me.

Courage in Action

Courage helped me overcome a literal obstacle. But what exactly is courage?

Courage is that place where you actually act on your convictions, even if that means going against the norm. It's also the place where you know there is going to be an outcome that is either positive or negative, and you choose to embrace both. You choose to move forward and act the best way you can in that moment.

Courage is important because it allows us to take that next step forward in our lives.

Life requires that we interact with people, that we grow, learn, and have new experiences. Without courage, we would just sit there, unspoken for. We would let things happen to us instead of making them happen. And that tends to lead us into name-blame-judge.

It takes courage to move forward, to stay in the situation

all the way to recognize-embrace-connect. However, when we do persevere with courage, we have one of the key pieces to succeed not just in the veterinary industry, but in life. We know that the situation might hurt and it's not going to be easy. But we can get through it.

Courage helps us get perspective, balance risk with action, and overcome negativity.

The Plank

Sometimes it can be hard to see the flowers through the weeds. But even though the risks we face in life can look like weeds, when we use courage to address them, we suddenly find that we can see them for the flowers they were all along.

One of the obstacles I encounter during Tough Mudders is called the Plank. This is a piece of wood two stories up. For this obstacle, you have to walk the plank and jump into the water. It's high up. You have to jump into muddy water, and you can't see the bottom. It can be intimidating.

By the fifth time I ran the Tough Mudder and encountered this obstacle, I was comfortable with the jump. When I got to the edge on this day, however, and was almost ready to jump off, I looked to my right and saw a woman, frozen. She just stood there with her hands at her sides, not moving, staring at the water below her.

I stopped what I was doing and went to help her. "You don't have to do this," I said. "No one will force you to, and no one will judge you if you don't."

Without looking away from the water, she answered, "I know. But I really want to."

She seemed to see only a field of weeds. So I told her about "fear-demand-choice." She was in a place where she was frozen in *fear* because she felt the *demand* to do this. She needed to frame it as a *choice* of whether she wanted to do it or not. Her fear was fed by the risks involved. So we talked about them.

"Can you swim?" I asked.

"Yes."

"Good, because you are going to have to swim." She

chuckled and made eye contact with me. "Have other people jumped in this water and gotten out?" I asked. "Is it deep enough?"

"Yes."

"Is there somebody in scuba gear already in the water, who is prepared to go in and get you if you don't come up right away?" I asked her.

"Yes."

"Is someone standing behind you with a gun, telling you that you have to do this?" I asked. "Does somebody have guns on your family, telling you that you have to do this or they'll all die?"

She laughed again. "No."

"That's because it's a choice," I replied, as I looked straight in her eyes. I told her that those questions all voiced demands, and they all said that she had to do it. But in reality, she had a choice. She could bypass the obstacle. Or she could recognize the risks, embrace them, connect with the situation, and move forward.

And she did. In fact, we jumped in together, spreading our arms and legs like starfish to stop from sinking too far when we hit the water. When her head broke the surface after we came up again, she was so happy. She now saw a whole *field* of flowers. She almost couldn't believe that she had done it.

You are not defined by your fear. Fear is something we create in our heads because we recognize risks. Courage means coming to grips with embracing risks, figuring out how to minimize them, and taking action so that you are able to succeed.

The Courage Not to Act

Sometimes having courage means deciding *not* to act.

In November of 2014, I was chosen to be part of a Tough Mudders special group to test the new obstacles for the coming year's Tough Mudders events around the world. I'd been through a few Tough Mudders by then. The point of this group was to test every new or adjusted Tough Mudders obstacle and give feedback about the reality of doing them on a course.

The catch was that I still had to be aware of my connective-tissue disorder.

I remember seeing King of the Swingers for the first time—that same leap from two stories up onto a trapeze bar that I went on to master later. But that day, I wasn't prepared for it. I could tell just from looking at it that doing this obstacle could seriously injure me.

At the same time, I could feel the pressure to do it from all the people around me. We were here to test the course. We had committed to doing *every* obstacle.

That morning, I faced down my fear that people would judge me, that they wouldn't think that I was worthy of being there—and I bypassed the obstacle.

If people did judge me for that decision, they didn't say it. Later, I did another obstacle better than a number of others—thus, in my mind, justifying my presence at the testing event. And in 2015, the same courage I used to bypass King of the Swingers became my driving force for overcoming it.

Fear comes from true risk, and it will always be there. Manage your decisions to act—or not act—with courage.

Retroactive Courage

Sometimes things go wrong, and that negativity can stay with us. When we face these situations, we have to have the courage to overcome them and get back to work again.

The very first patient I ever lost because of my decisions and the actions that followed was a seal-point domestic shorthair cat with a blocked urinary tract. I was a recent graduate, working under someone else, and I really felt like I had no idea what I was doing. We had limited resources to determine the risk factors for this cat. But the decision we made to go forward ultimately caused the death of the cat. I will never know whether that cat would have made it if we had taken a different path.

That cat died on my watch, under my hands. That truly sucked, but then it got worse. I had to pick up the phone and call the owners. When they had left the hospital earlier, the cat had been alive, and they were going to come back and get it and all would be okay. But I had to tell them that wouldn't happen. You never know how people are going to respond. These clients happened to be very understanding, and they went a long way toward helping me recover from that incident.

But I knew I would never forget that moment.

I went through all the stages of grief. Worse, the experience scarred me for other cases. My self-confidence had been completely rattled.

I held on to that shame for almost another year. And then another cat, an orange tabby, came in with the exact same scenario—a blocked urinary tract.

This time, I was the lead doctor. I had nobody to lean on, nobody else to go to. I could have gone to name-blame-judge—feeling like a failure and thinking how my boss didn't have my back with the first case. But I didn't.

I dug deep to move forward, and I approached the situation differently. I used what I had learned from my first experience. And this time, I saved the cat's life.

During the second procedure, the fear never went away. But because I faced it down with courage, I was able to recognize it and move through it. When you do that, fear can never stop you.

Conviction for my belief in helping animals drove me to want to take the step. Acceptance of my past judgment error, through recognition of my self-worth, allowed me to find the courage to actually take it.

Find Your Own Solution

One thing I learned from starting the 1 Life Connected movement is that I have to have the courage *not* to give people solutions.

I stand on stage, painting a picture and hoping the audience understands. But I don't want to tell them how to fix their lives, because they have the ability to do it themselves. People don't need me to fix them.

You don't need me to fix you, because in the end people don't need to be "fixed." I can't give you courage either, because you already have it. You have the courage to find a solution for yourself and speak up for your life, in any situation. Dig deep for it, and it will serve you well.

You have already walked a long way across the bridge back to connection. But you aren't on the other side yet. Acting with courage is powerful, but before you can harness all of its strength, you need to know how to connect with mindfulness. Empathy is the next piece in the connection puzzle.

Chapter 6

The Power of Empathy

The Brown Gauze Moment

Brown gauze taught me how to become empathetic toward myself.

It was a busy day at a very busy hospital. I saw forty-five to fifty patients, and I had that day that all veterinarians dread. Three people called in sick. The dental machine broke, and the only person who knew how to fix it was one of the people out sick. Therefore, we were behind in getting our anesthesia procedures started. And then we had three unexpected and significantly sick pets come in.

"Dr. Pope, can you look at this blood work?" "Dr. Pope, the x-ray light is broken." "Dr. Pope, can you talk to the husband and explain everything that you just told the wife?" "Dr. Pope, the computer up front just crashed!"

I hadn't eaten, or had anything to drink, or even gone to the bathroom all day. It felt as though I had just blinked and fourteen hours had flown by. Every time some new problem came up, I thought I wouldn't be able to make one more decision, or handle one more disaster. Somehow, though, I made it through the day.

I still had five or six more hours of notes to write, but at least no more people calling "Dr. Pope." All I had left to do was one bandage change on a kitten with a non-displaced fracture.

The kitten himself was doing great, and the bandage change was just to make sure he had the full time to heal. Normally, a registered technician would handle the actual bandage change, but since they were all out, I had to do it myself. I got my bandage tote. Inside I had regular gauze, vet wrap, Elastikon tape, bandage scissors—everything I needed to change his bandage.

Everything except brown gauze.

I needed the brown gauze to secure the cast padding. We used it for a lot of things at this hospital—securing endotracheal tubes, attaching e-collars onto dogs' collars, emergency muzzles. And of course, we used it for bandages. "All right," I told myself, "No problem. There's got to be some brown gauze around here somewhere."

I told my team to get me some. They told me we didn't have any . . . and the order for more wouldn't come until Tuesday, four days from now. I told them to *find* some. To appease me, they looked again, but they came back empty-handed. We just didn't have any.

In that moment, I sank to the bottom of my shame ocean.

"I'm nothing," I thought to myself. "I'm worthless. I can't do this bandage the way I'm supposed to. I'm not doing right by this patient. How can I say that I run a hospital if I can't even stock enough brown gauze? *We have to have brown gauze.*"

I stormed to the back of the hospital and yanked open every single cabinet and drawer in the treatment area. I pulled everything out and threw it onto the counters and the floor. Still no brown gauze.

Then I looked around at what I had done.

It looked like a tornado had hit the hospital. I came out of the moment. I gathered myself. I went back to the kitten and finished the bandage change without the brown gauze. And thankfully, my team members understood why I had turned into a human wrecking ball and destroyed the back of the hospital.

Going forward, any time one of my team members recognized that I was starting to sink or needed to fill one of my balloons, they left a little piece of brown gauze on my desk by my computer. That was my hint that I needed to eat or go pee or take a deep breath.

That was the signal that I had permission to take care of myself.

Connect to Empathy

Every single person has had a brown gauze moment. If you are able to recognize, embrace, and connect with my story, congratulations: you have found empathy.

Empathy is being able to connect with emotions instead of judging or ignoring them, whether for yourself or for someone else. Teresa Wiseman, a nursing scholar in England, explains the four concepts of empathy as the following: One is to see the world as other people see it. Two is to see that other people have emotions. Three is to not be judgmental. And four is to be able to vocalize those emotions back.

The hardest part about empathy is just recognizing the world as it is. The world is not out to get us. Empathy is also about learning to accept ourselves while realizing that it's not all about us, individually.

Empathy doesn't exist when we fall into the ocean of shame and let all the negativity come in. When we decide not to be empathetic and to disconnect, we put a wall around ourselves. This is when our lives become unspoken. We become lonely and isolated, even from ourselves.

And the critical piece to recognize is that we can't have empathy for others if we don't have empathy for ourselves.

We may think we're being empathetic, but really we're own-ing others' pain instead. When we own their pain, we name it, blame it, and judge it, and in the end, we can't allow true empathy to show up.

When we recognize, embrace, and connect with emo-tions, however, then we are all one again. It comes back to balancing the positive and the negative: the negative emo-tions exist, but the positive ones also come out. As soon as we become aware of both, we are able to connect with another human and say, "You are worthy of being here. I believe in you, and I care about you. This situation really sucks, but we're in it together. Let's take a step forward and see where it goes."

Many people think that being empathetic means we give up ourselves to be there with the other person, but I don't believe that's true. In fact, first we have to have empathy for ourselves, which includes having self-empathy in the face of caregiver's guilt. Then we can have empathy for others and connect with them through communication, both verbal and nonverbal. And finally, we can learn to have empathy with society as a whole. That will allow us to see that empa-thy can be both positive and negative.

The Shame Antidote

As veterinarians, we live with caregiver's guilt every day. It is a reality of our world, no matter how you look at it. We have to work harder to find self-empathy through that guilt, before it sinks us into shame.

Guilt and shame are closely related. The difference, according to researcher Brené Brown, is that guilt is what we feel for things we *do* and shame is more about who we *are*. As noted in chapter 1, Brown defines shame as having the experience of believing we're unworthy of acceptance and belonging. Even though guilt is different from shame, left unchecked, guilt can quickly become a sinker that drags us deep into the ocean of shame.

I like to examine this idea of guilt and shame through the hypothetical example of a cat that comes in with a disease that can't be cured.

For whatever reason, we know that we cannot cure the cat, no matter what we do. We could do an abdominal ultrasound to find out a little bit more about what's going on inside the cat. This may give us an idea of how long the prognosis might be, or it can tell us whether we can give additional pain meds to make the cat more comfortable. It's not going to change the progression of the disease, but it may give us more information. However, the cat is going to hate it. Claws will come out, teeth will be bared, and it will be stressful to put the cat through this.

Caregiver's guilt is going to come no matter what in this situation. If we don't do the ultrasound and the cat dies, we say to ourselves, "You should have done the ultrasound." On the other hand, if we do the ultrasound and the cat still dies, we say to ourselves, "You should not have done the ultra-sound." We have guilt over our actions because we could not change the outcome.

What is the difference between guilt and shame? If we don't do the ultrasound, shame makes us say to ourselves, "Who are you to call yourself a veterinarian? You don't try hard enough; you're not doing everything you possibly can for that cat. You don't deserve to be a vet. You don't deserve to be here!"

On the other hand, if we *do* the ultrasound, our shame tells us, "Who are you to call yourself compassionate? You put that cat through an unnecessary procedure. The cat hated it, and it was painful, and you made that cat suffer more than it needed to. You don't deserve to be a vet. You don't deserve to be here!"

Instead of feeling guilt over actions, we sink into shame. And instead of just questioning our actions, we question our very beings.

So what is the antidote to shame? According to Brené Brown, it's empathy.

When we're in a negative bias, as happens with care-giver's guilt, we are going to name-blame-judge. And that shows up toward ourselves as much as it shows up toward other people. But we can't have empathy for others unless we first have empathy for ourselves.

We have to recognize our guilt, without allowing it to sink us into our ocean of shame. In learning to embrace the situation, we recognize it is part of being a caregiver. Through that struggle, we then find a path to self-empathy—which brings us back into connection with ourselves and with others.

Empathy for Others

It can be easy for us to be negative about how other people handle situations. Empathy for others helps us recognize that if the situation sucks, we're still able to live with the other person and be okay with it.

When I was in practice, a guy brought in a kitten with a broken leg—a dark-point Siamese. The kitten was really sweet and had a great attitude. Even with a broken leg, he tried to attack a toy ball.

This guy didn't have the money to fix his kitten's leg, so he wanted to euthanize the cat. My team thought he was such a jerk. They immediately went to name-blame-judge. "Why can't he see that he *has* to take care of his cat?" they asked. "He just has to come up with the money somehow."

In some ways, I agreed with them. The man had made a commitment to this kitten when he took it in. But I tried to step away from judging him. He was afraid. He wanted to give up. It was easier to let this cat die, and then maybe get another one. I lived in that space with him and accepted his perspective. I didn't agree with it, but I was able to understand how he saw things.

Then I told him that I would not euthanize the kitten. I told him that if he was going to go home and kill the cat or let it die, he could leave it with us, and we would surrender it to the Humane Society. And I told him that he had a third option, too. He could take the kitten to the emergency clinic to find out what they said. They had payment options with outside credit-support companies, and maybe one would work for him. I reminded him that there were other people who could help.

In the end, he elected to go to the emergency hospital, to at least hear what other options he had. The clinic worked with him on payments through a credit service, and he ended up doing the surgery. This man, whom we had all judged, chose to keep his cat. He just needed someone to see him and be with him in a space of empathy.

Here is the true power of empathy, though: if he had elected not to do that, I would have accepted him either way.

We all have fear inside of us. That's part of being human. But we all have empathy, too. True empathy shows up when we recognize our own humanity through others.

Career Counseling

Empathy is a critical piece of strong communication—and connection.

A lot of people ask me whether I think they should

become veterinarians. It can be difficult to remember to be empathetic when answering them.

It is tempting to tell them, "No! Run! It's not worth the money. It's not worth the stress. You're going to hate it." Many of us want to tell them how horrible it is. And it can be really bad. People would be appalled by some of the things we deal with in a hospital setting. I once heard a story about a dog that got its tongue stuck in a shredder. I've seen a horse that had its tongue ripped out by another horse because they were fighting over food. As vets, we see really graphic things and negative situations on a daily basis.

But me going on a rant is not going to solve anything for the people asking me whether they should become vets. Instead, I need to find a place of empathy.

I need to connect with them, have a conversation, and try to understand what it is they love about the idea of veterinary medicine. They don't see the world as I see it, because they've never experienced the negativity that comes with being in the medical field. When I take the time to see the world the way they see it, however, I can be empathetic for the hope and joy that they have. That allows me to connect with them emotionally. Then I can give them a more balanced, honest answer about the profession—one that will help them make the right decision for them.

When you can empathize with people, they can hear your side and you can relate to theirs. You can communicate in a clear way without an ulterior agenda. You can connect.

The Plane Question

I have found that, as veterinarians, we sometimes hold ourselves to unrealistically high standards. And our ability to work with empathy gets even more complicated when we factor in society's view of us.

I fly a lot in sharing the message of 1 Life Connected, and whenever I travel, I sit next to people who ask what I do for a living. I tell them I'm a speaker, and that I speak on well-being in my industry. Then I quickly turn it back to them and ask what they do, so that I don't have to answer any more questions.

Once in a while, though, people follow up and ask more about my industry.

At that point, I have to be honest. "I'm a veterinarian," I tell them with a sigh. I know what is coming next. "Why do veterinarians need motivational speakers?" So I let them know. Veterinarians have a very high suicide rate. There is a lot of burnout, and many of us are very discontented with our careers.

The other passenger always gets a very quizzical look on his or her face. Almost all of them say, "Really? I thought you all loved animals. I thought you all love what you do." If only it were all that easy.

The truth is that pressure from society is what causes a lot of our discontentment. We as caregivers are put on a pedestal we cannot live up to. We can't always be the person we are expected to be. And when we're not, we feel that we have failed both ourselves and society.

Society has an idealistic vision of veterinarians because of the value of the human-animal bond. People value that bond, and that drives their vision of us. They put us on a pedestal because of how much we value it, too. If their connection to that bond did not exist, they would not feel the need to help their pets—and we couldn't help those pets either.

When we name-blame-judge society for putting us on a pedestal, we no longer regard the value of that bond. We need to recognize and embrace their vision of us because, without it, we wouldn't have the jobs that we do. We wouldn't be able to help the animals that we are so committed to.

We don't have to agree with their vision, or the pressure it puts on us. We just have to empathize with it and move forward.

Lose Your Cool

Think about the last time you had your own brown gauze moment, when you completely lost your cool, whatever that might look like.

Remember the environment you were in. What sinkers pulled you down? What balloons did you need to refill? What made you feel unspoken for? Recognize the emotions you felt. Don't judge them. There is nothing wrong with you getting so frustrated that you cause your own little tornado. Even if you are the chief of staff, you are not unworthy because you lost your cool one time. Or twice. Or three times.

Each of us needs to accept that it's okay to lose our cool. It doesn't mean that we are bad people. It just means that we *are* people. I have had to coach individuals through their own brown gauze moments. I help them to embrace their emotion and then find a path to connect through empathy for themselves. When we can embrace our emotions and connect with them, we can move forward.

Show yourself that empathy. When you do, you'll be able to truly connect with others and be empathetic for them, too.

Empathy is another big step across the bridge to a connected life. But you can't go all the way if you don't know how to weather the constant ups and downs of this work. With resilience, the next step, you can keep moving forward.

Chapter 7

Stronger, Faster, Better: Connect through Resilience

Speech Interrupted

In fall of 2016, I gave a speech at a team-building event for 1 Life Connected, through the sponsorship of a pharmaceutical company. I spoke about balloons and sinkers, name-blame-judge, and recognize-embrace-connect. I talked about what being connected is like, for me, as a veterinarian and a speaker.

During the whole talk, one particular person in the room was extremely negative.

She worked in the industry but wasn't a veterinarian. And she didn't agree with me. "You're too negative," she yelled, while I was actually up there talking. "You paint such a negative picture." Even though she was demonstrating that very picture right then, I let her words in. I translated what she said to mean that I was a negative person, and that I come from a bad place.

I started to sink.

As she kept shouting out comments and interrupting me, other people in the room started to talk. They asked her to be quiet. They had been embracing the 1 Life Connected message, and now this woman was taking them away from it. They wanted to be able to hear, but she didn't allow them that space.

She was sinking everyone around her.

That was when I realized that this was the time to really live the 1 Life Connected message. I needed to recognize and embrace the situation. So I took a breath, stopped my speech, and looked right at her. I told her that I understood her perspective, and that it was okay that she didn't agree with what I had to say. But there were people in the room who wanted to hear the message, and we all needed to respect that.

After that, she quieted down, and I was able to continue my talk. I connected with the people in the room who needed to hear the message, whether or not she became one of them.

I didn't name, blame, or judge her for her actions, because I recognized that I didn't know what was driving her response. What I did know was that it wasn't a direct attack to my value or worth. And because I knew that, I was able to keep her negativity from dragging me down.

Strength in Resilience

I was able to recover and move forward with sharing the message of 1 Life Connected because I am resilient.

When we walk across the bridge of connection, over the darkness, both negative and positive things swirl around us. Resilience is being able to hold both of them, yet keep moving forward.

Sinkers occur, and sometimes we can't stop them. So instead of allowing ourselves to go unspoken for, we lift ourselves up with our balloons and recover. Each time we do this, it makes us more resilient to the next sinker. Resilience is our ability to take a push toward the side of negativity but lean back into the positive again afterward.

Resilience is important because sinkers are always going to be there. We can have self-worth, and we can have the conviction to work through them. We can have the courage to act, and we can have empathy to be present for them. But if we can't find resilience to keep moving forward in the long term, we will eventually sink back into an unspoken-for life.

Resilience is something we need to use constantly. All day long we sink, we fill our balloons, and we bounce back. It's not easy, but we have to continue to recognize-embrace-connect. When we do, we find the path back to connection. Resilience gives us the strength to keep connecting, every day, even when we want to give up.

Resilience can show up for us as physical, mental,

emotional, and spiritual strength. Resilience is the air in your balloons.

One More Mile

Any time I run a Tough Mudder, I rely on physical resilience. There is always a moment, in each race, when I have to dig deep and find some push to make it to the finish.

One year, I participated in a Tough Mudder that took place in the mountains of Whistler, Canada. We were at a high altitude, and the day started out beautiful, warm, and sunny. As we moved through the obstacle course, though, a cold front came in. It started to rain.

At first it wasn't that bad. But the water they used in the obstacles was from the mountain.

I wasn't prepared for how cold it was.

One of the obstacles was called the Mud Mile, and it was a series of trenches filled with that icy water from the mountaintop snowmelt. I was in it for a long time, and it froze me to the core. I was wet and cold. My lips turned blue, and my fingers didn't work. I knew I couldn't stop moving because my muscles would seize up.

And then came the Arctic Enema—jumping straight into a container of ice water.

That was where I finally paused. I had to ask myself, "What is more important: doing the Arctic Enema, or being able to finish the race?" I recognized that I was already at my limits, even without that obstacle, and I skipped it.

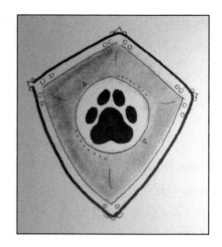

But the damage had already taken its toll. I was cold. I was wet, and tired, and miserable. I was done.

For a minute, I considered dropping out.

Instead, my physical resilience kicked in. I told myself to do one more step, then one more mile. I was still able to do Everest, a big half-pipe I had to run up as the last obstacle of the event. I was able to finish the race.

I have run more than ten Tough Mudders, as well as other mud runs and half marathons, since 2013. And they have all been brutal. People often ask me why I do these events, especially with my EDS. As I said earlier, I do them because they restore my faith in humanity. And I do them to push through the physical, mental, and emotional struggle.

I do them because my resilience says I can, and therefore I will.

My First Day

Resilience can also be mental. With physical resilience, you just keep moving. With mental resilience, you don't give up.

I learned the power of mental resilience my very first day as a veterinary intern.

After four years of undergraduate studies, a year of research, and then four more years of medical school, I was ready. I had my own truck for the ambulatory part of the business. I had my own business cards, my own desk, my degree on the wall, and my license framed in the front office.

All the pieces were finally in place.

I walked into the clinic that day with bright eyes and a grin from ear to ear. This was my first day as a veterinarian, and I was going to make a difference. I was ready.

I found one of my bosses. And he immediately handed me two 60-cc syringes of pink fluid.

Of course I knew what they were. But I couldn't respond. I just looked at him. So he made it very clear. "Go euthanize the horse in the back," he said.

I had euthanized horses when I was in school, so this wasn't the first time. That wasn't the problem. And I'm sure there was a valid reason that he gave that task to me when he did. But it still meant that my very first act as a veterinarian would be to go out and take a life.

Part of me wanted to say, "Seriously, screw this and screw you!" To my boss.

But I knew this moment wouldn't define the rest of my career. The fact was, I was a veterinarian. And euthanasia was part of the job. I didn't name-blame-judge my boss. I tried to recognize-embrace-connect with what I had to do.

We were a full-service hospital, and if this was the action needed for this horse at this time, I had full faith that we had done everything we could for him. I would be able to provide the horse with the good death and remove his suffering.

When I returned to the office after finishing the deed, my smile wasn't as big. My eyes weren't as bright. I was a little subdued, because it had taken something out of me. It sunk me a little bit.

I told myself it would get better after the internship. It would get better when I started a new job. It would get better when I reached the next point. I was wrong about all of those things.

Because when you get to that next point, you realize something: it doesn't *get* better—you *make* it better. You keep going. You don't give up. You play a tough mental game.

You are resilient.

The Tuberose Candle

Like physical and mental resilience, emotional resilience keeps you afloat above your shame ocean.

Earlier, I touched on euthanasia. I consider euthanasia both one of the most wonderful and one of the most painful things I can do as a veterinarian. When I'm euthanizing an animal, even if it's the "logical" thing to do from a medical perspective, it can be a truly beautiful gift for both the animal and its owner. However, because of the emotional situation, it still takes a toll on me, and that sinks me a little bit.

In 2003, I found something that helped me recover from this sinker and others like it: a tuberose candle.

I kept this candle in my desk drawer, next to my computer. I never lit it in the hospital. It was really small. I chose tuberose because when I got married in Hawaii, I wore a tuberose lei. Whenever I had to go through a hard situation such as euthanasia that emotionally drained me, I went back to my office area afterward, opened the desk drawer, and smelled the candle.

Right away, the scent took me back to my wedding day: the beach, the salt in the air, the closeness of my family, the love I felt making that commitment to my husband—and of course, the smell of the tuberoses around my neck. I remembered all of that and felt an honor for love and life that immediately made me feel better. Then I'd close the drawer and return to my day.

Emotional resilience is a big part of staying engaged with

what we do. Whatever you need to do to fill your emotional-resilience balloon, take the time to do it.

A Ten-Mile Run

Resilience isn't just physical, mental, and emotional. It's also spiritual.

When I feel disconnected spiritually, I know that I need to go outside and be exposed to nature. That allows me to connect with the world and be spiritually involved with not just my own energy, but also the energies around me. When I recognize that I'm having a hard time, I know that being outside keeps me from sinking.

Sometimes, a nudge from a teammate or colleague reminds me to fill my spiritual balloon, because I need that resilience.

In 2015, I worked for a pharmaceutical company that launched a revolutionary dermatological product that was going to change the way the profession managed pruritus ("itch") in dogs. Pruritus is a very common issue, and dermatology is a huge part of veterinary care. The problem came when I was told that we had a short supply. And it took two years to make the product.

When we realized that we hadn't made enough, there was no way to fix that problem in quick order.

I was on a call with my team when I heard how much higher the demand was than the supply available. There would be a shortage, more than previously thought. That meant I would have to call all the veterinary dermatologists in my market, to tell them that they would have to choose which dogs to take off of the product. Many of these dogs didn't have other options, and because they were so bad off, there was a good chance they would have to be euthanized. How do you choose who lives and who doesn't?

I knew these conversations would be horrible. My hands immediately clenched, and my eyes closed. I felt my spirits sink. And my team recognized that. They knew that I filled my spiritual balloon by running on the beach. Trying to lighten the situation, someone joked, "This will be a ten-mile run for you, Kim!"

We all laughed, but I put my running shoes on right away.

Before I could do anything, I needed to go outside and recover from getting that terrible news. I knew I was going to have to share that message with my colleagues. I knew the pain they would go through and the empathy they would feel in telling their clients they couldn't get this drug. I needed to fill my balloons, to recover my resilience, before I could do that and come up with creative ideas to help them find solutions.

And in the end, that's what happened. The situation was still hard. But we made it through, and for me, a big part of staying connected during that tough time was my spiritual resilience.

Spiritual resilience affects a bigger network than just you. It allows you to connect with your profession as a caregiver, as well as everyone touched by that care. When you see how you are connected to everything, and how you affect the bigger web of connectedness, you can see how important it is to fill your spiritual-resilience balloon.

Practice Resilience

Resilience looks different for everyone. Different things try to knock us from our paths, just as different things help us fill our balloons.

Some people do meditation to reinforce their resilience. Others go to a therapist. I like to run, spend time with animals, and be out in nature. And I have to practice those things every day. They are the fuel that fills my balloons.

But like a gas tank, filling your balloons one time won't last forever.

We have to keep filling them, even when it's difficult, and especially when we are feeling unspoken for. A sinker might grab us by one hand as we hold a balloon in the other, and we still have to keep going. Every time we succeed in taking one more step forward, we become more resilient.

You have now built your bridge to connection with self-worth, conviction, acceptance, courage, empathy, and resilience. The only thing left is to view that connection at a higher level. The last piece of connection is vision.

Chapter 8

A Vision of Connection

Touch a Life

In 2014, I was asked to do a well-being lecture at Oklahoma State University. I expected parts of it to resonate with the veterinarians and technicians present. But I had no idea how deeply it would touch one particular life.

In my talk, I spoke about veterinarians having a high risk for suicide. An older gentleman asked me, "Who are you to say that we have a high risk of burnout or suicide? I don't think that's true." I didn't judge him for his opinion. But I let him know that if this talk resonated with somebody in the room, then it was worth it for me to share that message.

After I finished giving the lecture at Oklahoma State, a woman came up to me. She was around my age and about my height, with a pale complexion and blond hair partly pulled up into a ponytail.

There were tears in her eyes.

She looked at me and said, "You have no idea what this lecture has done for me. You probably never will, but you have changed my life." And she turned and walked away, crying, just as someone else approached me.

I tried to find her to speak with her further, but she had disappeared into the crowd.

That was the first time I recognized that the 1 Life Connected message I have been given the power to share is so much bigger than me. It's about other people and what they do with it.

As I continue to share this message with the world, I find that a handful of people still come up to me after every talk. Some e-mail me later. But I know that for every one or two who tell me that the 1 Life Connected message made a difference, there are another three, or four, or five who are also affected.

I don't give solutions. I just paint a picture. And I remind them, "You're normal. There's nothing wrong with you. Go out and live."

The Vision to Connect

That picture I paint when I speak is part of my vision.

Vision recognizes that there is something bigger than each of us, as individuals. It is larger and more encompassing than just the place or the situation we are in. With vision, we are able to own the overall picture.

All living creatures have two things in common, no matter what other differences we may have: we are all born, and we all die. Without vision, we just exist and wait for death to come, our lives unspoken for. We don't have a clear focus or a direction to go in. Vision gives us a place for our energy to move toward. It provides us a reason to get up and go to work, beyond just making money to buy food and pay for a house, eat and then shit in that house, and then clean up the house—only to repeat it all the next day. Ultimately, our vision is the destination that we are driving toward.

Vision brings you to life, because once you find it and hold on to it, it gives you inspiration. At the same time, you bring your vision to life by choosing to feed it and share it with others. As you share it, other people influence your vision, and it grows.

This is the ultimate connection. This is the spoken life at a higher level.

My Vision

Within about two years of my turning point—the day I decided not to take my own life—I was able to start living my vision.

I decided I would no longer live in a space where my actions would be defined by somebody else. I wanted to live in a place where my actions were for other people, for connection. I wanted to be present.

So I became a minimalist. My husband and I downsized significantly. We stopped spending money on stuff and started spending it on experiences instead. We got out. We started to see the world.

And as I started to reconnect with the world, I started to reawaken.

At some point along that path, I came across a quote by Albert Einstein that helped me to define my personal vision:

A human being is a part of the whole, called by us the "Universe," a part limited in time and space. He experiences himself, his thoughts and feelings, as something separated from the rest, a kind of optical delusion of his consciousness. This delusion is a kind of prison for us, restricting us to our personal desires and to affection for a few persons nearest to us.

Our task must be to free ourselves from this prison by widening our circle of compassion to embrace all living creatures and the whole of nature in its beauty. Nobody is able to achieve this completely, but the striving for such an achievement is in itself a part of the liberation and a foundation for inner security.

This quote embodies my personal vision because it shows me the value of where I'm going.

We all have to make sacrifices in our lives. We are able to lean on the first six of the seven principles of connection—self-worth, conviction, acceptance, courage, empathy, and resilience—to move forward. But it is the seventh principle, vision, that shows us the bigger picture of what we truly believe in.

I believe in life. I believe life is beautiful. And because of my vision, I know that we are all 1 Life Connected, to each other and to the universe.

Embrace Imperfection

We go through a lot of things in our industry, and it's hard. So many things pull us into the shame ocean, and it's very difficult to take the time to fill our balloons. Sometimes, we do start to move toward that very dark, negative abyss.

But when we pull ourselves back from that abyss through recognize-embrace-connect, it not only makes us stronger veterinarians; it actually makes us stronger in life, as well.

Now, when I deal with hard situations outside of veterinary practice, I am more resilient. Before, when I isolated myself with name-blame-judge, I was just me—one life. By learning to change my perspective and going to recognize-embrace-connect, I became part of something that was bigger than me again.

I became 1 Life Connected.

Staying connected sometimes means embracing imperfection. We have to embrace a space where we can accept that our careers and lives are going to ask more of us than we can ever give. Our inability to do everything does not define us. The outcomes of situations we can't control don't define us. It's what we *are* able to focus on and move forward with that makes the real difference.

My journey from name-blame-judge to recognize-embrace-connect hasn't been easy. It is not as though I woke up one day and everything was rainbows and unicorns. I still work at it every day. But I wouldn't trade what I've learned about life from the struggle of being a veterinarian.

I am a much stronger person now, because of it. Being a veterinarian taught me so much about how to live life.

Find Your Path

If you are ready to build your own bridge to a connected life, you may be wondering, "How do I start?"

The answer to *how* is "yes."

Say yes to life. Start with the decision you make when you find yourself hanging on by your fingertips and you reach out to grab a balloon. Start by pulling yourself up and giving yourself permission to find the path to your sustainable life.

The ability to do all of this is already inside you. But you don't have to do it alone.

You can find someone to help you work through this process. Maybe you need someone to talk to. There are life coaches, therapists, and psychiatrists. Maybe you need to physically move through it. You can find yoga instructors or fitness and health coaches. There are meditation coaches. Sometimes medications are needed to help balance chemicals in our brains. Maybe the best resource for you is a spiritual leader.

The important thing is to recognize what kind of space helps you fill up your balloons, and then find the resources to match. Only you know which resources will make the biggest difference to you. Once you find them, don't be afraid to just dig in.

You can even connect with the 1 Life Connected movement. We have support tools available for you, Including worksheets that have step-by-step questions and activities to help you figure out how this message of connection shows up for you in your life specifically. You can access this free resource and many others on the website at 1lifecc.com.

The resources within 1 Life Connected and beyond can help you get started on the path to connection. You have permission to take the first step: the ball is in your court.

The Other Side

By recognizing, embracing, and connecting with self-worth, conviction, acceptance, courage, empathy, resilience, and vision, you have all the tools you need to build your personal bridge back to connection. You are ready to begin your journey. As you do, I want to leave you with one last message: You are normal. There is nothing wrong with you. You don't need to be "fixed."

Negative vibes will show up, but they don't define who you are. You can't ignore them, but you can partner with them and still find the positives. You can balance out the sinkers and the balloons, and you can move forward from name-blame-judge to recognize-embrace-connect.

You can transform your unspoken life into a life that has a voice.

Recognize each of the characteristics in this book and find them within yourself. You have the ability to use each of them to pull yourself through any struggle.

You deserve to be here. You deserve to be a part of this world.

You belong. And you are one life connected.

Now go out and live!

ABOUT THE AUTHOR

Dr. Kimberly Pope-Robinson is a sought-after speaker and the founder of 1 Life Connected. She has served in the veterinary field for more than twenty years. After graduating from the UC Davis School of Veterinary Medicine in 2000, she practiced in both the large and the small animal sectors. In 2007, Dr. Pope transitioned into a leadership position for a corporate veterinary practice, and then to a position in the pharmaceutical industry, where she worked with veterinary specialists and colleges of veterinary medicine. During this time, Dr. Pope supported hundreds of veterinarians and their teams.

Dr. Pope's career experience provided her with a unique exposure to the stresses of the veterinary profession. This gave her a strong understanding of the lack of fulfillment often found in the profession. Since then, Dr. Pope has worked to help others manage their perfectionist tendencies, confront their personal shame, and develop the skills of self-forgiveness and resilience. These became cornerstones of 1 Life Connected, through which veterinarians build the foundation for a sustainable career in the industry.

A dynamic speaker, Dr. Pope shares the 1 Life Connected message around the country, helping others to stay connected with their life's passion through their careers. She and her husband of fifteen years, Jeff, live in San Clemente, California, with a variety of furry and feathered friends.

ABOUT THE ARTIST

Matthew Salaiz is a veterinary practice manager who has been an active member of the veterinary field since he was fourteen years old. He is passionate about making an impact in the veterinary field through community service, by facilitating, coordinating, and participating in various activities.

Salaiz "fills his balloons" with art and music, as well as with outdoor activities such as hiking, camping, and fishing. His biggest "balloon-filler," however, is the love of his pet Pancho, who posed as the loose model for the illustrations in this book. California natives, Salaiz and Pancho live in the Central Valley.

MARKETING PAGE

Are you ready to cross the bridge back to connection?

1 Life Connected offers resources to help you on your journey, including:

- Free worksheets and support to help you navigate the message on your own
- A member-supported community of connected veterinarians and caregivers
- Videos, forums, and other resources for individual veterinarians and teams
- Thirty-day "balloon" finding and filling challenges, to get you started
- Customized support to bring you and your team back to connection

You can also connect with Dr. Kimberly Pope-Robinson through:

- In-person speaking engagements for your organization
- Life coaching to recognize, embrace, and overcome challenges
- Retreats with like-minded veterinarians on the path back to connection

To learn more, visit www.1LifeCC.com, or call (916) 847-4807.